Venison

Fast and Foolproof Favorites

WILLOW CREEK PRESS

Minocqua, Wisconsin

Venison

Fast and Foolproof Favorites

RECIPES FROM THE READERS OF *Sports Afield*

EDITED BY HENRY SINKUS

WILLOW CREEK PRESS

Minocqua, Wisconsin

© 2003 Willow Creek Press
Illustrations © Clipart.com

Design: Katrin Wooley

Published by Willow Creek Press
P.O. Box 147, Minocqua, Wisconsin 54548
www.willowcreekpress.com

Library of Congress Cataloging-in-Publication Data

Printed in Canada

Table of Contents

Soups, Stews and Casseroles 11-35

Chops and Roasts 37-71

Baked Breaded Venison Chops—64
Chicken-Fried Venison Steak—65
Hawaiian-Style Venison Chops—66
Venison Roast with Bacon & Onions—67
Roasted Rack of Venison—68
Grilled Venison Tenderloin—69
Venison Sauerbraten with Gingersnap Gravy—70

Ground Venison 72-99

Venison Meatballs with Rice—74
Venison Meat Loaf—75
Texican Venison Chili—76
Venison Meatballs with Water Chestnuts—77
Venison & Mashed Potato Pie—78
Venison Lasagna—79
Texican Venison Lasagna—80
Venison Mediterranean—81
Barbecued Venison Meat Loaf—82
Venison Gravy & Biscuits—83
Venison Meat Loaf with Craisins—84
Venison Meat Loaf with Peppers & Onions—85
Venison Meat Loaf with Andouille Sausage—86
Oriental-Style Venison—87
New England-Style Venison Chili—88
Crockpot Venison Sloppy Joes—89
Venison Cabbage Rolls—90

Miscellaneous Venison Recipes 101-113

Appetizers, Side Dishes, Sauces, and Other Recipes 115-135

Index 143-144

Soups,
Stews
and
Casseroles

Texas Venison Stew

1 lb. course ground venison
2½ cups raw cubed potatoes
1 cup chopped onion
1 can condensed tomato soup
1 15-oz. can red kidney beans
1 tsp. salt
⅛ tsp. pepper
2 Tbs. chili powder
4 cups water

In a heavy skillet, sauté the onion until tender. Add venison, chili powder, salt and pepper, and cook until the meat is well browned. In a 4-quart saucepan, combine the kidney beans with the potatoes and water; bring to a slow boil and cook until the potatoes are tender. Add the tomato soup and the venison to the saucepan; stir well and simmer one hour.

Serves 4.

Henry says: "This a great recipe for hunting camp, quick and easy."

Venison Chunk Chili

1½ - 2 lb. venison, cut into ¾-inch chunks
2 medium onions, diced
2 15-oz. cans tomato sauce
2 15-oz. cans stewed tomatoes
1 large green pepper, diced
2 Tbs. chili powder
1 tsp. salt
⅛ tsp. red pepper
1 tsp. oregano
1 or 2 cans kidney beans

 In a medium stockpot, brown the venison and onions in 2 Tbs. oil. Add the tomato sauce, stewed tomatoes, green pepper, chili powder, salt, red pepper and oregano.

Simmer covered over low heat for 2 hours. If not thick, remove cover for the last 20 minutes of cooking. Add the kidney beans just before serving and heat through.

Serves 6.

Henry says: "Add some diced dried fruit to your chili for that gourmet touch."

Venison Succotash Stew

2 lb. venison cut into ¾-inch cubes
4 slices thick bacon cut into 1-inch pieces
¼ cup flour
¾ tsp. salt
2 medium red potatoes, thinly sliced
2 15-oz. cans stewed tomatoes
1 10-oz. package frozen lima beans
1 12-oz. can whole kernel corn
1 chicken bouillon cube
3 cups hot water

In an 8-quart Dutch oven, cook the bacon over medium heat until browned. Remove bacon and drain on paper towels. Spoon off all but 2 Tbs. of the bacon drippings.

Combine the flour and salt, and coat the venison cubes. Cook the venison in the bacon drippings until brown.

Add potatoes, tomatoes, corn, lima beans, bouillon, and 3 cups of hot water. Bring to a boil over high heat; reduce heat to medium and cook 10 minutes or until venison and vegetables are tender. Sprinkle each serving with crumbled bacon.

Serves 4 to 6.

Henry says: "A great recipe for the busy family where no one eats at the same time. Make this recipe a day ahead, portion in individual bowls, and re-heat as needed."

Venison Vegetable Pie

1½ cups venison cut into ½-inch cubes ⅓ cup flour
1 cup red potato, diced
1 cup onion, chopped
1 tsp. celery seed
1 tsp. garlic powder
1 tsp. seasoned salt
¼ tsp. fresh ground pepper

⅓ cup flour
2 Tbs. butter plus 1 tsp.
1 14-oz. can chicken broth
1 8.5-oz. can diced peas and carrots
1 cup button mushrooms, sliced
1 box chilled pie crust, at room
      temperature

 In a heavy skillet, melt 1 Tbs. butter and sauté the venison cubes, onions and mushrooms until the meat is brown. Set aside to cool.

In a large saucepan, over medium heat, melt 2 Tbs. butter and then whisk in 1 tsp. butter until smooth. Add the chicken broth and juice from the peas and carrots; whisk until thickened. Add the potatoes, peas and carrots, meat mixture, and seasonings; stirring constantly, heat until thick and bubbly.

Line a 9-inch, deep-dish pie tin with one pre-made pie crust. Using a slotted spoon, transfer the meat/vegetable mixture to the pie shell. Moisten the bottom pie crust edge, and place the second crust on top; crimp seal the edge. Cut vent slits in the top crust. Bake in a preheated 400° oven for 30 to 40 minutes; the pastry will be nicely browned. Let the venison vegetable pie set for 30 minutes to facilitate easy serving.

Serves 4 to 6.

Henry says: "A wonderful make-ahead meal. Store several in the freezer. Add ⅓ cup red wine for a more robust flavor."

Venison Camp Stew

2 lb. boneless venison cut into 1-inch cubes
2 can beef consommé
1 cup red wine
4 - 5 carrots, peeled and cut into ¼-inch rounds
3 medium white onions, coarsely chopped
2 turnips, peeled and cut into ½-inch dice
1 small head cabbage, cored and coarsely chopped
4 medium red potatoes, cut into ½-inch dice
2 bay leaves
4 Tbs. sweet or unsalted butter
½ tsp. salt
¼ tsp. white pepper
½ tsp. beau monde

In a 12-inch cast iron Dutch oven, melt enough butter to cover the bottom. Season the venison with salt, pepper, and beau monde; sauté the venison until brown on all sides. Add consommé and red wine to just cover the meat and simmer, covered, for 30 minutes. Add the carrots, onions, turnips, cabbage, and bay leaves. Cover and simmer for 1 hour, then add the potatoes and simmer for 30 minutes, or until the potatoes are tender.

Serves 4 hungry hunters.

Henry says: "Adding some steak sauce will give sparkle to the sauce. Watch the level of the liquid while simmering; add additional consommé and/or red wine to keep everything covered."

Sweet and Sour Venison Stew

1 lb. venison, trimmed of all fat and cut into bite-sized pieces
1 medium white onion, cut into 8 wedges
2 medium potatoes, cut into ¾-inch dice
2 medium carrots, peeled and cut into ¾-inch dice
1 medium green pepper, cut into ¾-inch pieces
1 cup tomato sauce
¼ cup Sauternes wine
¼ cup apple cider vinegar   Dry Rub Mixture
1 cup brown sugar   ½ cup flour
1 cup water   ¼ tsp. white pepper
1 tsp. dried basil   ¼ tsp. onion powder
½ tsp. garlic salt   ½ tsp. garlic salt
4 Tbs. peanut oil   dash of cinnamon

Roll the venison in the Dry Rub Mixture. In a 10-inch heavy skillet, heat the peanut oil over medium heat, add the onion and brown. Add the venison and sauté until brown. Drain off excess oil, add Sauternes, tomato sauce, vinegar, water, and brown sugar; stir to mix thoroughly, cover, and simmer over low heat for 20 minutes. Add potatoes, carrots, green pepper, basil, and garlic salt; adjust seasoning with salt and pepper. Cover and simmer for 30 minutes or until vegetables are tender.

Serve over steamed rice.

Serves 4.

Henry says: "In a classic stir fry, the venison would be cut in thin strips, and the vegetables thinly sliced and quickly fried in a very hot wok. This recipe works well, but using traditional techniques produces better results."

Venison Apple Pot Pie

3 cups cubed venison loin
½ cup chopped onion
3 Tbs. olive oil
1 can condensed cream of chicken soup
1 large granny smith apple, peeled, cored and cubed
⅓ cup craisins (dehydrated cranberries)
1 Tbs. lemon juice
¼ tsp. black pepper
dash of salt
pastry for single crust pie

In a heavy skillet, heat the oil and sauté the venison until cooked through. With a slotted spoon, remove the venison and drain on paper towel. Add onions to the skillet and cook until tender, 2 - 3 minutes. Remove from heat.

In a large stainless bowl, combine the venison, onions, soup, apple, craisins, lemon juice, salt and pepper. Spoon the mixture into a 9-inch, deep-dish pie pan. Place pie crust over mixture and crimp fold the edge; cut three steam vents. Bake in a preheated 425° oven for 30 - 35 minutes or until crust is brown and filling is bubbly.

Serves 4.

Henry says: "A great dish for those late fall dinners, or a wonderful addition to a buffet."

Creamy Venison Stew

2 lb. boneless venison, cut into bite-sized cubes
3 medium potatoes, peeled and cubed
1 cup carrots, peeled and sliced
½ cup chopped onions
1 pint heavy cream
1 cup milk plus 1 cup water
1 tsp. coarse ground pepper
1 tsp. garlic salt
2 Tbs. olive oil
2 Tbs. flour
3 Tbs. butter

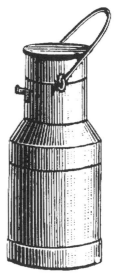 In a Dutch oven or crockpot, heat the olive oil and brown the venison and onions. Add the potatoes, carrots, milk and water, and salt and pepper. Simmer for 3 to 4 hours or until vegetables are tender.

In a small saucepan, melt the butter and whisk in the flour over medium heat. Continue to whisk until the rue is light brown in color, then whisk in the heavy cream to make a smooth sauce. Add the sauce to the venison/vegetable mixture and stir to combine. Continue cooking until thickened and heated through.

Serves 4 to 6.

Henry says: "Can be made ahead and refrigerated for a day or frozen. If reheating from frozen, thaw in the refrigerator for 24 hours."

Venison Crockpot Stew

2 lb. venison cut into 1-inch cubes
2 medium onions, chopped
3 stalks celery, sliced
3 medium red potatoes, cut into 1-inch cubes
6 carrots, peeled and sliced ⅜-inch thick
1 slice white bread, cubed
1 15-oz. can stewed tomatoes
1 Tbs. brown sugar
1 Tbs. teriyaki sauce
1 tsp. salt
¼ tsp. pepper
1 cup water

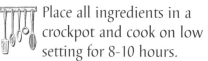 Place all ingredients in a crockpot and cook on low setting for 8-10 hours.

Serves 4 to 6.

Henry says: "Add ¼ tsp. garlic, and another root vegetable like rutabaga or parsnips, for added flavor. Additionally, a more robust flavor can be achieved by substituting red wine for the water called for in the recipe."

Venison Potato Casserole

1 lb. coarse ground venison
½ cup chopped onion
2 Tbs. peanut oil
4 large baking potatoes, peeled and sliced ¼-inch thick
½ cup chopped celery
2 Tbs. dried celery leaves
1 10-oz. can cream of mushroom soup
½ cup heavy cream
1 Tbs. Worcestershire sauce
½ tsp. salt
¼ tsp. white pepper

In a 4-quart saucepan, heat the oil and brown the venison and onion. Add the chopped celery and celery leaves and sauté for 5 minutes. Stir in the soup, cream, Worcestershire, salt and pepper, and remove the pan from the heat.

Grease a 2-quart casserole dish and layer one-half of the sliced potatoes on the bottom. Spoon one-half of the venison mixture over the potatoes, then a layer of the remaining potatoes, topped by the venison mixture.

Bake covered in a preheated 400° oven for 1 hour, or until the potatoes are tender.

Serves 4 to 6.

Henry says: "Great comfort food. For a tasty variation, try substituting 2 sweet potatoes for 2 of the baking potatoes."

Crockpot Venison Barbecue

2 lb. boneless venison, cut into 1-inch cubes
4 slices bacon, cut into ¼-inch strips
1 cup chopped onions
1 cup chopped green pepper
1 15-oz. can tomato sauce
½ cup red wine vinegar
4 Tbs. brown sugar
1 Tbs. chili powder
2 Tbs. Worcestershire sauce
2 cloves garlic, minced

In a heavy skillet, fry the bacon until brown; remove and drain on paper towel. Add the venison and brown on all sides. Add the onion and sauté for 5 minutes. Transfer the venison and onion to a crockpot and stir in all remaining ingredients. Cover and simmer on low heat for 3 to 4 hours. Serve over steamed rice or on bakery fresh buns.

Serves 6.

Henry says: "In our test kitchen, we found that this barbecue was much better if made a day ahead and re-heated. It can also be frozen; another make-ahead meal for the family or hunting camp."

Venison Barley Stew

1 lb. ground venison
1 medium onion, chopped
3 stalks celery, chopped
3 cups tomato juice
1 cup water
¼ cup pearl barley
¼ cup fresh parsley, chopped
1 tsp. chili powder
½ tsp. salt
¼ tsp. white pepper
¼ cup craisins
    (dehydrated cranberries)

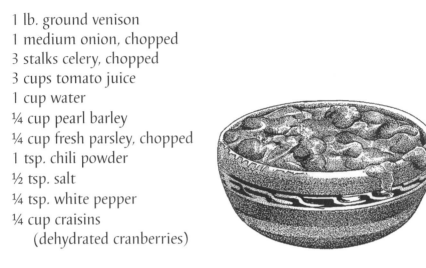

In a 4-quart saucepan, cook the venison, onion, and celery until the meat is no longer pink. Stir in the tomato juice, add the parsley, water, barley, chili powder, salt and pepper, and bring to a boil. Reduce heat to simmer, cover, and cook for 40 to 50 minutes or until the barley is tender.

Serves 4.

Henry says: "In the test kitchen, we added craisins to add sweetness to this dish. Further, if you use a vegetable-blended tomato juice, you will produce a more rounded flavor."

Venison Broccoli Stew

2 lb. venison cut into ¾-inch cubes
½ cup flour
½ tsp. salt
¼ tsp. pepper
3 Tbs. olive oil
2 medium onions, sliced
2 large carrots, sliced
3 cups broccoli florets
1 cup fresh mushrooms, sliced
3 cups chicken stock or broth
1 cup heavy cream

In a large bowl, combine the flour, salt and pepper. Add the venison and toss to coat evenly. In a large Dutch oven, heat the oil and brown the venison on all sides. Add the chicken broth, onions, and carrots, and bring to a boil. Reduce heat to medium, cover, and simmer 1 hour. Add the broccoli and mushrooms, and stir in the heavy cream. Cover and simmer for 15 minutes or until the broccoli is tender but still crisp.

Serves 4 to 6.

Henry says: "The original recipe called for condensed cream of broccoli soup, which is convenient, but we used fresh broccoli and heavy cream with wonderful results."

Hunters Venison Casserole

2 lb. boneless venison, cut
   into ¾-inch cubes
½ tsp. salt
¼ tsp. pepper
2 large red onions, chopped
1 lb. whole fresh button mushrooms
3 carrots, peeled and sliced
3 medium red potatoes, sliced

2 green peppers, chopped
1 15-oz. can stewed tomatoes
1 cup red wine
1 cup chicken stock
2 Tbs. cornstarch, dissolved
   in the chicken stock
1 lb. mostaciolli noodles, cooked
1 lb. mozzarella cheese, shredded

In a heavy 4-quart saucepan, heat 1 Tbs. olive oil and brown the venison on all sides. Add the onions and carrots; cook until the onions are translucent. Add the mushrooms, potatoes, green pepper, wine, and stewed tomatoes and simmer for 30 to 40 minutes or until potatoes are just tender. Stir in the chicken stock/cornstarch mixture and heat until thickened.

Butter a 4-quart casserole dish; begin with a layer of noodles, followed by a layer of venison/vegetable mixture, followed by one-third of the cheese. Repeat the layering twice more. Bake in a preheated 350° oven for 35 to 40 minutes or until cheese is brown and bubbly.

Serves 6.

Henry says: "The original recipe contained only venison, carrots, and potatoes, cooked in a pot on top of the stove, which was okay, but not very interesting. Make this one day ahead for a fast, easy, and delicious dinner."

Venison Goulash

2 lb. venison, cut into 1-inch cubes
¼ cup butter
2 medium onions, peeled and chopped
2 large green peppers, seeded and cut
    into 1-inch strips, 2-inches long
4 small potatoes, peeled and cubed
½ tsp. salt
1 Tbs. sweet paprika
2 15-oz. cans stewed tomatoes

In a 4-quart Dutch oven, heat the butter and brown the venison on all sides. Add the onions and sauté until the onions are transparent. Add the green pepper, salt, and paprika, and stir in the stewed tomatoes. Cover and simmer over low heat for 25 to 30 minutes. Stir in the potatoes, cover, and simmer until the potatoes are tender. Serve over fresh noodles.

Serves 6.

Henry says: "A wonderful dish for those wintry evenings when you dine by the fire."

Venison and Wild Rice Stew

1 lb. venison, cut into 1-inch cubes
1 lb. pork sausage, cut into ½-inch pieces
1 large white onion, chopped
4 cups cooked wild rice
2 cups fresh mushrooms, sliced
3 - 4 cups heavy cream
½ cup chopped celery
2 cups chicken stock or bouillon
1 tsp. sweet basil
½ tsp. salt
¼ tsp. white pepper

In a heavy skillet, brown the venison and pork sausage on all sides. Add the onion and celery and sauté until the onion is translucent. Transfer this mixture to a 4-quart Dutch oven; add the mushrooms and chicken stock, cover, and simmer over low heat for 20 minutes. Add the cooked wild rice, basil, salt and pepper, and stir in 3 cups of heavy cream; cover and simmer for 15 minutes. Add remaining cream and adjust seasoning with salt and pepper.

Serves 6.

Henry says: "A meal that's in between a soup and a stew. Add more liquid for a delightful cream soup; add vegetables to make a hearty stew."

Italian Venison Stew

3 lb. venison, cut into 1-inch cubes
1 large onion, coarsely chopped
3 cloves garlic, crushed
¼ cup fresh parsley, chopped
1 Tbs. dried rosemary, crushed
4 bay leaves
4 - 6 peppercorns
4 whole cloves
2 cups red wine
½ cup red wine vinegar
¼ lb. butter
2 10-oz. cans stewed tomatoes
1 cup pitted black olives
2 cups quartered artichoke hearts

 In a large stainless steel bowl, alternate layers of venison with the onion, garlic parsley and spices. Add wine and wine vinegar, cover bowl, and refrigerate for 48 hours. (If marinade does not cover meat, add more wine and vinegar in a 4-to-1 ratio.) After refrigeration, drain the venison, and strain and reserve the marinade.

In a 4-quart Dutch oven, braise the venison in the butter. Add the tomatoes, olives, and artichoke hearts with 1¼ cups of marinade. Cover and simmer over low heat for 20 minutes or until venison is tender. Serve over fresh pasta or noodles.

Serves 4 to 6.

Henry says: "Now that's Italian! Add zucchini squash and/or lima beans during the last 10 minutes of cooking for added flavor and texture."

Venison Barley Soup

1 lb. coarse ground venison
½ cup quick cook barley
2 15-oz. cans chicken broth
1 15-oz. can tomato puree
2 packages frozen mixed vegetables
2 Tbs. Worcestershire sauce
3 Tbs. steak sauce
1 Tbs. brown sugar
2 Tbs. butter

In a 4-quart stockpot, melt the butter and brown the venison. Stir in the tomatoes, barley, and chicken stock. Heat to boiling, stirring occasionally. Add the Worcestershire, steak sauce, brown sugar and stir well, then add the vegetables. Reduce heat and simmer, covered, for 10 to 15 minutes or until barley is tender.

Serves 4 to 6.

Henry says: "A quick and easy soup; if you do not like barley, substitute fine noodles or rice. If using rice, it is advisable to pre-cook the grain."

Venison Broth

3 lb. venison shank, cut 2 inches thick
4½ quarts cold water
2 carrots, peeled and cut into 2-inch pieces
1 small turnip, peeled and cut into quarters
4 stalks celery, cut into 2-inch pieces
1 whole onion, peeled and stuck with 4 cloves
1½ tsp. salt
3 sprigs fresh parsley

In a large stockpot, one that will fit in your oven with the lid, combine the water and venison shank, and bring slowly to a boil. Skim off both fat and foam. Add the vegetables, salt and parsley. Bring the mixture to a boil and skim off fat and foam again.

Cover and place in a preheated 350° oven. Bake slowly for about 3 hours. The broth should be clear and golden amber in color.

To serve, ladle broth into bowls and offer venison and vegetables on the side.

Serves 6.

Henry says: "Time consuming but worth the effort. Serve with a hearty red wine and crusty French bread."

Venison Burgundy

6 strips thick-sliced bacon, cut into ¼-inch pieces
2 lb. venison loin, cut into thin strips about 2-inches long
¼ cup flour seasoned with ¼ tsp. salt and a dash of pepper
4 small onions, cut into 1-inch dice
1 - 2 cloves garlic, minced
1 10-oz. can beef consommé
2 lb. fresh button mushrooms
2 cups Burgundy or Cabernet wine
¼ cup chopped parsley
¼ tsp. rubbed thyme
¼ tsp. marjoram
¼ lb. sweet or unsalted butter

Preheat oven to 300°.

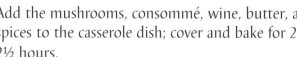 In a large heavy skillet, brown the bacon; remove with a slotted spoon and drain on paper towel. Dust the venison with the seasoned flour and brown on all sides in the bacon drippings. Transfer the venison with a slotted spoon to a 4-quart, oven-proof casserole dish.

Using the same skillet, melt one-half of the butter and brown the onions and garlic; transfer to the casserole dish.

Add the mushrooms, consommé, wine, butter, and spices to the casserole dish; cover and bake for 2 to 2½ hours.

Serves 4 to 6.

Henry says: "Add a little brandy to enhance the flavor, and serve over noodles or mashed potatoes."

Venison Stroganoff

2 lb. venison loin, sliced thinly and cut into 2-inch long pieces
¼ cup flour, seasoned with ¼ tsp. salt and a dash of pepper
1 lb. button mushrooms
¼ lb. sweet or unsalted butter
1 15-oz. can stewed tomatoes, chopped
   or pureed in a food processor
2 cloves garlic, minced
1 pint sour cream
3 Tbs. Worcestershire sauce

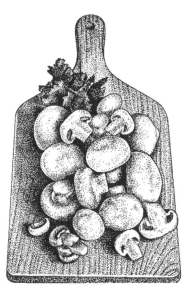

Dust the venison with the seasoned flour. In a heavy skillet, melt one half of the butter and brown the venison on all sides. With a slotted spoon, transfer the venison to a 4-quart oven-proof casserole dish.

Melt the remaining butter and brown the onions and garlic; add these to the casserole dish along with the mushrooms.

Blend together the stewed tomatoes, sour cream, and Worcestershire sauce, and gently stir into venison mixture.

Cover and bake in a preheated 325° oven for 1 to 1½ hours.

Serves 4 to 6.

Henry says: "This recipe can be frozen, but omit the oven cooking and the sour cream. Complete these steps when finishing the dish."

Venison Pasta Casserole

1 lb. venison steak, cut into ½-inch cubes
1 tsp. dried basil
¼ tsp. pepper
⅛ tsp. garlic powder
2 cans golden mushroom soup
1 15-oz. can stewed tomatoes, chopped
2 cups frozen mixed vegetables
1 cup shredded sharp cheddar cheese
½ lb. ziti pasta, cooked and drained

Preheat oven to 400°.

 In a large sauté pan, brown the venison in olive oil. Stir in all remaining ingredients, except the pasta and cheese, and heat through.

Transfer mixture to a large bowl and combine with the pasta. Spoon the mixture into a 2-quart, buttered baking dish and cover with the cheese. Bake uncovered for 20 to 30 minutes, or until the cheese is melted and the mixture is hot and bubbly.

Serves 4 to 6.

Henry says: "Another make-ahead entrée that can be frozen. Add a few red pepper flakes or perhaps green chili to add additional spark to this dish."

Teriyaki Venison

2 lb. boneless venison, cut into 1-inch cubes
½ cup teriyaki sauce
1 clove garlic, minced
2 Tbs. light brown sugar
2 Tbs. sherry wine
2 - 3 Tbs. olive oil
2 - 3 green onions, chopped

 In a stainless steel or ceramic bowl, combine the teriyaki, garlic, sugar, sherry, and green onions. Add the venison, stir, cover, and refrigerate for 24 hours.

Drain the venison, and reserve the marinade. In a heavy skillet, heat the oil and brown the venison on all sides. Add the reserved marinade and heat through.

Serves 4 to 6 as an entrée, 6 to 8 as an appetizer.

Henry says: "If you are using the recipe as an entrée, serve over rice. As an appetizer, serve with crusty sour dough baguette slices."

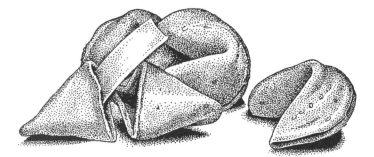

Hungarian-Style Venison Goulash

3 lb. venison, cut into 1-inch cubes
¼ cup butter
3 medium onions, peeled and chopped
3 large green peppers, seeded and cut into 1-inch strips, 2-inches long
½ tsp. caraway seeds
½ tsp. salt
1 Tbs. sweet paprika
2 cups sour cream

In a 4-quart Dutch oven, heat the butter and brown the venison on all sides. And the onions and sauté until the onions are transparent. Add the green pepper, salt, paprika, and caraway seeds. Cover and simmer over low heat for 25 to 30 minutes. Stir in the sour cream and simmer until heated through. Serve over fresh noodles.

Serves 6.

Henry says: "A wonderful dish; add more paprika if you like it spicier."

Chops
and
Roasts

Brandied Venison Loin

1 boneless venison loin, cut into 1-inch medallions
2 cups brandy
2 cups peach or apricot juice

<u>Dry Rub Mix</u>
1 Tbs. salt
1 Tbs. paprika
¼ tsp. granulated garlic
¼ tsp. white pepper

 Dust the venison loin slices with the dry rub mix, cover, and refrigerate for 1 hour.

In a stainless steel bowl, mix together the brandy and apricot juice. Add the venison, cover, and refrigerate for at least 4 hours.

Remove the venison from the marinade and either pan fry or grill to the desired degree of rareness. Serve with steamed vegetables and new potatoes, crusty bread, and a bottle of red wine.

Serves 4 to 6.

Henry says: "The longer the venison marinates, the more flavor it captures. When frying or grilling, be careful not to burn the venison; this marinade contains sugars that will burn. Additionally, oil your grill or skillet to avoid excessive sticking."

Barbecued Venison

1½ lb. venison back straps, cut into 1-inch-thick slices
1 cup flour
1 tsp. pepper
1 Tbs. seasoned salt
5 Tbs. olive oil

Mix together the flour, pepper and salt. Coat the venison with the seasoned flour on all sides. In a heavy skillet, heat the oil and brown the venison on both sides. Remove from heat and place in a Crockpot or slow cooker.

Barbecue Sauce
1 cup red wine vinegar
¼ cup Dijon mustard
1 cup molasses
¼ cup ketchup
2 Tbs. Worcestershire sauce

 In a medium-sized bowl, whisk together all ingredients. Pour over venison, set the Crockpot on low, and cook for 6 to 7 hours.

Serves 4.

Henry says: "During the last 2 hours of cooking, add thick-sliced onions for added zest and flavor."

Filet of Venison Wellington

4 6-oz. venison filets
6 mushrooms, finely chopped
1 Tbs. butter, softened
1 clove garlic, finely chopped
9 squares prepared puff pastry dough
1 egg, beaten
¼ tsp. seasoned salt
¼ tsp. white pepper

Mix together the mushrooms and butter. Season the filets with a blend of seasoned salt and pepper and let stand 15 to 20 minutes.

Roll out 4 squares of puff pastry to double in size. Roll 4 additional squares to 1⅔ size.

Place a filet on a 1⅔-size square of puff pastry, spoon 1½ Tbs. of mushroom and butter mix on top, and brush the edge of the pastry with beaten egg. Cover with a double-size piece of puff pastry and press-seal the edge. Trim excess pastry 1 inch from the filet and crimp seal. Brush the pastry package with beaten egg and cut 4 decorative patterns from the remaining square of puff pastry. Place a decoration on top of the pastry package and brush with beaten egg. Repeat the process for the remaining filets.

Bake the Wellingtons in a preheated 400° oven for 35 to 45 minutes or until the pastry is golden brown.

Serves 4.

Henry says: "A formal presentation that is well worth the time and effort. Serve with fresh steamed vegetables and new potatoes."

Crockpot Venison Tenderloin Roast

3 whole venison tenderloins
½ cup Dijon mustard
¼ cup bourbon
¼ cup teriyaki sauce
2 Tbs. Worcestershire sauce
¼ cup brown sugar
½ cup green onion, chopped

Place the tenderloin in a crockpot. In a bowl, mix together the remaining ingredients and pour over the tenderloin.

Cook on medium for 4 to 4½ hours.

Remove the tenderloins and let sit for 10 minutes. Slice the tenderloins, and arrange on a serving platter topped with the sauce from the crockpot.

Serves 6 to 8.

Henry says: "Add pearl onions and baby new potatoes to the crockpot the last hour of cooking, along with 2 cloves of peeled whole garlic".

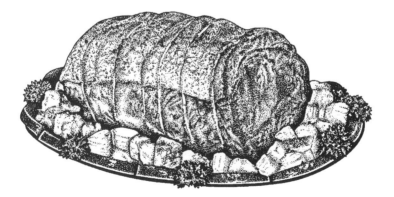

Venison with Spinach and Peppers

6 venison chops, grilled to rare
1 large red pepper, cut into ¾-inch strips
1 large yellow pepper, cut into ¾-inch strips
1 large red onion, cut into ½-inch wedges and separated
3 Tbs. olive oil
½ tsp. salt
¼ tsp. pepper
1 cup fresh orange juice
2 Tbs. red wine vinegar
1 Tbs. honey
¼ tsp. red pepper flakes
8 cups washed, trimmed, and
    dried fresh spinach leaves

 Preheat the oven to 425°. Place peppers and onion in a 13"x9"x2" baking dish, dust with salt and pepper, and bake for 15 minutes. Stir in one-half of the orange juice and layer the chops over the peppers and onion. Cover and bake for 15 minutes.

In a 1-quart saucepan, mix the remaining orange juice with the vinegar and honey, bring to a boil, and reduce the mixture to 2 Tbs.

Toss the spinach with the orange, vinegar, and honey reduction and transfer to a serving platter. Top the spinach with the chops and pepper and onion.

Serves 6.

Henry says: "Formal, simple and elegant. Add a bottle of Cabernet wine and who knows . . ."

Venison with Brandy and Cream

6 venison steaks, grilled to rare
8 shallots, sliced thin
1 cup carrots, peeled and sliced ¼-inch thick
¼ lb. sweet butter
6 slices thick-cut bacon, cut into ½-inch strips
½ cup brandy
1 cup chicken broth or bouillon
2 cups heavy cream
¼ cup prepared horseradish
½ tsp. salt
¼ tsp. white pepper

In a heavy skillet, melt the butter and sauté the shallots until translucent. Add the bacon and sauté until brown. Increase the heat and carefully add the brandy; when flame dies add the chicken stock and carrots, then stir in the cream and

salt and pepper. Reduce heat and simmer until the carrots are fork tender. Stir in the horseradish and simmer 5 minutes.

Place chops in a baking dish, pour over the shallot/carrot sauce, cover and bake in a 350° oven for 35 to 40 minutes.

Serves 6.

Henry says: "Serve with fresh cranberry sauce and wild rice."

Pan-Fried Venison Steak

6 boneless venison steaks, cut ½-inch thick
½ cup flour seasoned with ½ tsp. salt and ¼ tsp. pepper
4 Tbs. olive oil
4 large potatoes, peeled and sliced
1 large onion, peeled and sliced
1 cup carrot, diced
1 cup mushrooms, sliced
1 cup heavy cream

Dredge the venison steaks in the seasoned flour. In a heavy oven-proof skillet, heat the oil and quickly brown the steaks on both sides. Remove the steaks from the skillet, layer the vegetables on the bottom of the skillet, and add the cream. Return the steaks to the skillet, cover, and place in a preheated 325° oven for 1½ to 2 hours, or until vegetables are tender.

Serves 4 to 6.

Henry says: "Experiment with other vegetables such as squash or eggplant for variety. Cooking can be completed by simmering on the stovetop, but check to insure cream does not evaporate."

Barbecued Venison Chops

8 boneless or bone-in venison chops, cut ½-inch thick
1 cup teriyaki sauce
¼ cup molasses
¼ cup orange juice
2 cloves garlic, minced
1 medium onion, minced fine
2 Tbs. sugar

 In a stainless or ceramic bowl/container, mix together the teriyaki, molasses, orange juice, garlic, onion and sugar. Cover and refrigerate for 24 hours.

Preheat your outdoor grill to medium high.
Grill the chops 4 minutes on each side, basting the chops on both sides with the sauce. The venison will be on the medium-rare side but will not be dry.

Serves 6 to 8.

Henry says: "This barbecue sauce works well for poultry as well as pork. This sauce has a very high sugar content, so be alert and avoid burning."

Grilled Marinated Venison Chops

5 lb. boneless or bone-in venison chops, cut ½-inch thick
1 cup teriyaki sauce
¼ cup soy sauce
8 cloves garlic, minced
6 shallots, minced fine
4 Tbs. brown sugar
1 tsp. sesame seeds

 In a stainless or ceramic bowl/container, mix together the teriyaki, soy, garlic, shallots, sugar and sesame seeds. Add the venison chops, cover and refrigerate for 24 hours.

Drain marinade from the venison chops and wipe off any excess moisture. Preheat your outdoor grill to medium high. Grill the chops 4 minutes on each side; the venison will be on the medium rare side, but will not be dry.

Serves 6 to 8.

Henry says: "This marinade works equally well for poultry, pork and beef. This marinade has a high sugar content, so be alert and avoid burning."

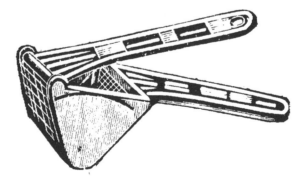

Barbecued Venison Tenderloin

2 whole venison tenderloins

Barbecue Sauce
2 oz. Grand Marnier liqueur
¼ lb. sweet butter
2 shallots, finely minced
1 clove garlic, minced
¼ tsp. oregano
¼ tsp. cumin

¼ tsp. salt
2 Tbs. chili powder
2 cups catsup
¼ cup molasses
¼ cup red wine vinegar
1 cup orange juice

Barbecue Sauce:

In a 3-quart saucepan, melt the butter over medium heat. Add the shallots and garlic and sauté until the shallots are translucent. Add the dry spices and continue cooking for 2 to 3 minutes, stirring constantly. Add the catsup, molasses, vinegar, orange juice, and Grand Marnier; mix thoroughly. Reduce heat, cover and simmer for 1 hour. Store finished sauce in a covered container under refrigeration.

Barbecued Tenderloin:

Place the venison tenderloins on a sheet of buttered heavy-duty foil. Cover the tenderloins with 1 cup of barbecue sauce. Fold over the foil and seal. Place foil package on a hot outdoor grill for 20 to 30 minutes or place in a preheated 350° oven for 40 minutes. Remove package from heat and let sit 15 minutes before slicing. Serve with fresh vegetables and steamed new potatoes.

Serves 4 to 6.

Henry says: "This sauce is citrus-based with orange flavors; try lemon, lime or apricot, but change the liqueur to an appropriate flavor."

Roasted Venison Hindquarter

1 venison hindquarter trimmed of all fat
    and sized to fit your roasting pan
¼ lb. sweet butter
4 to 6 medium onions, peeled and quartered
6 large peeled carrots, cut into 1-inch pieces
6 to 8 medium-sized potatoes, peeled and cut into quarters
½ cup craisins (dehydrated cranberries)
3 15-oz. cans stewed tomatoes
2 cups Cabernet wine

Melt the butter in the roasting pan on the stovetop and brown the venison on all sides. Pour the stewed tomatoes over the venison, add the wine, cover the roaster and bake in a preheated 350° oven for 20 minutes per pound. During the last 45 minutes of baking, add the onions, carrots, and potatoes. Internal temperature for the venison roast should be 180°.

Remove venison to a carving platter and place vegetables in a covered dish and keep warm. Pour the liquid from the roaster into a saucepan, and purée with a stick blender; add wine if necessary. Adjust seasoning with salt and pepper. Heat to almost boiling, then stir in 2 Tbs. butter and serve with your sliced venison roast.

Serves 6 to 8.

Henry says: "To add additional moisture to the venison, try covering the top of your roast with strips of thick-sliced bacon during the roasting process."

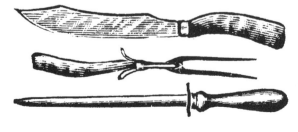

Roasted Venison with Onions and Peppers

1 boneless venison leg, cut into several pieces
3 large onions, peeled and sliced
3 cloves garlic, minced
4 stalks celery, sliced
3 carrots, peeled and sliced
6 large green peppers, cut into ¾-inch strips
½ lb. thick-sliced bacon, cut into 1-inch pieces
2 cups chicken broth or bouillon
¼ lb. sweet butter
¼ cup Worcestershire sauce
½ tsp. crushed rosemary
½ tsp. salt
¼ tsp. white pepper
1 cup dry white wine

Place a sheet of heavy-duty foil in a roasting pan; foil should be large enough to cover and seal the venison and vegetables. Place the venison in the roaster, season with salt, pepper, and rosemary. Add the onions, garlic, celery, carrots, green peppers, and bacon. Pour in the chicken broth, Worcestershire and wine; dot the top of the venison with dots of butter. Fold and seal the foil. Place roaster in a preheated 350° oven and bake for 3 hours or until meat is tender. Let roast stand for 15 minutes before slicing.

Serves 8.

Henry says: "We achieved excellent results cooking this roast a day ahead, slicing the venison and returning it to the cooking juice, resealing and refrigerating. Re-heat in a 300° oven for 1 hour; it will melt in your mouth."

Honey-Roasted Venison

3½ - 4 lb. boneless venison roast
1½ cups olive oil
7 Tbs. honey
7 Tbs. cider vinegar
1 cup teriyaki sauce
3 medium onions, peeled and chopped fine
3 cloves garlic, minced
1 tsp. ground ginger

Place the venison roast in a one-gallon storage bag that seals. In a medium-sized bowl, combine the remaining ingredients. Add one-half of the mixture to the venison; seal and refrigerate the venison for at least 4 hours or overnight. Cover the remaining marinade and refrigerate.

Drain the venison and discard the used marinade. Place the reserved marinade in a saucepan and bring to a boil, stirring occasionally; remove from heat.

Place the venison roast on a rack in a shallow roasting pan. Roast at 325°, basting frequently with the marinade, for 2 to 3 hours, or until tender and the internal temperature reaches 180°.

Serves 6.

Henry says: "Another roast that can be prepared a day ahead, sliced, refrigerated, and re-heated the next day".

Cranberry Venison Pot Roast

4 lb. boneless venison roast
4 cups cranapple juice
1 15-oz. can whole cranberry sauce
1 cup teriyaki sauce
1 medium onion, peeled and chopped fine
1 clove garlic, minced
¼ tsp. ground cloves

 Place the venison roast in a one-gallon storage bag that seals, and add 2 cups cranapple juice; seal and refrigerate the venison for at least 4 hours or overnight.

Place the venison roast in a 5-quart slow cooker. In a small bowl, mix the cranberry sauce with 2 cups cranapple juice, garlic, onions, and ground cloves. Pour the mixture over the venison roast; if necessary, add additional cranapple juice to cover the roast. Cover and cook on low 7 to 8 hours or until the venison is tender. Serve over hot rice or buttered noodles.

Serves 6.

Henry says: "Bursting with flavor, this roast is so tender it can be cut with a fork."

Boned Venison Roast with Bacon

3 - 4 lb. boned venison roast
1 lb. thick-sliced bacon
1 package dry onion soup mix
1 can beer
½ tsp. seasoned salt
¼ tsp. white pepper
3 Tbs. olive oil
2 cups mushrooms, sliced
4 medium potatoes, sliced thick

Butterfly-cut the boned roast and lay cut side up. Place bacon strips on the cut side of the roast, season with salt and pepper, and roll and tie the roast.

In a heavy Dutch oven, heat the oil and brown the roast on all sides. Add the dry soup mix and the beer, cover, and bake in a preheated 350° oven for 3 to 4 hours. During the last hour of cooking, add the mushrooms and potatoes.

Serves 6.

Henry says: "This recipe is straight out of our test kitchen; a bit of additional work, but well worth the effort."

Italian-Style Venison Shanks

Per serving:

1 lb. venison shank, cut into 2-inch slices
1 small onion, cut into 8 sections vertically
½ cup stewed tomatoes
½ clove garlic, chopped
¼ tsp. Italian seasoning
¼ tsp. sweet paprika
¾ cup red table wine
2 Tbs. red wine vinegar
or 1Tbs. balsamic vinegar
2 Tbs. olive oil
1 carrot and 1 medium potato,
    cut into bite-sized pieces

In a heavy sauté pan, heat the olive oil and brown the venison shank on both sides. Arrange the shanks in the pan in a single layer; add all the remaining ingredients, except the carrot and potato. Over low heat, simmer covered for 1 to 1½ hours, or until fork tender. The shanks should remain covered in liquid during the cooking process; add water or additional wine if necessary. Add carrots and potato during the last 30 minutes of cooking. Serve with Italian bread and a hearty red wine.

Henry says: "Best if made a day ahead and re-heated; provides a richer, more robust flavor."

Oriental-Style Venison Steak

2 lb. boneless venison steak, sliced ½-inch thick
1 cup green onions, thinly sliced
2 Tbs. sesame seeds
⅓ cup sesame oil
½ tsp. fresh grated ginger
1¼ cups teriyaki sauce
¾ cup water
1 Tbs. minced garlic
3 Tbs. brown sugar

In a ceramic or stainless steel bowl, create a marinade by mixing the brown sugar with the teriyaki; add the garlic, ginger, sesame oil and seeds; stir well and mix in the onions.

Place the venison slices in a plastic kitchen bag that can be sealed; pour marinade over the venison, seal and refrigerate for 24 hours.

Drain the marinade from the venison. Preheat an outdoor grill to medium-high and cook the venison for 1 to 1½ minutes on each side. Serve as an appetizer or over rice as an entrée.

Serves 4 as an entrée, 8 to 10 as an appetizer.

Henry says: "This is an incredible recipe, as close to Korean- or Hawaii-style beef as one dares."

Marinated Venison Chops

3 lb. venison chops, sliced 1-inch thick

Marinade
⅓ cup red wine vinegar
3 Tbs. olive oil
3 Tbs. teriyaki sauce
1 Tbs. Worcestershire sauce
2 Tbs. black strap molasses
1 tsp. dried tarragon
1 tsp. salt
1 tsp. Dijon mustard
1 tsp. fresh garlic minced
¼ tsp. white pepper

In a medium-sized stainless steel bowl, whisk together the ingredients for the marinade. Cover and refrigerate for 24 hours.

Place the venison chops in a single layer in a shallow, non-metallic pan and cover with marinade. Cover the pan and refrigerate for 4 to 6 hours.

Preheat an outdoor grill to medium-high and cook the chops for 2 minutes on each side. Place the chops in a baking dish and place them in a preheated 300° oven for 15 minutes.

Serves 6 to 8.

Henry says: "Serve with grilled fresh vegetables and roasted ears of corn. A great dish for a picnic."

Venison Scaloppine Provençale

8 boneless venison leg slices, cut ¼-inch thick and flattened to ⅛-inch thick
½ cup flour seasoned with ¼ tsp. salt and ¼ tsp. white pepper
1 Tbs. olive oil
1 tsp. butter
1 cup fresh mushrooms, sliced
1 medium cucumber, peeled, seeded and diced
2 fresh tomatoes, peeled, seeded and diced
2 Tbs. fresh chives, minced fine
1 clove garlic, minced
2 Tbs. Marsala wine

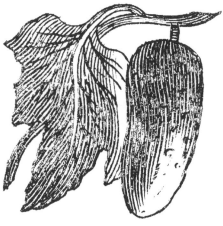

Dust the venison slices with seasoned flour. Heat the oil and butter in a heavy skillet. Sauté the venison quickly, browning both sides. Remove venison from skillet and keep warm.

Add mushrooms, cucumber, tomatoes, chives and garlic to the skillet, and sauté over high heat for 2 minutes. Add wine and blend well. Arrange the venison on a serving platter and cover with sauce.

Serves 2 to 3.

Henry says: "Best results are achieved when you heat your skillet to almost smoking, but be careful of spattering hot oil!"

Venison Pot Roast with Mushrooms

4 lb. boneless venison roast
2 cups Cabernet wine
2 cups chicken stock
1 medium onion, peeled and chopped fine
1 clove garlic, minced
¼ tsp. basil
2 cups button mushrooms, sliced
2 cups portabella mushrooms, sliced thick
1 cup heavy cream

Place the venison roast in a 5-quart slow cooker. Add wine, chicken stock, onion, garlic, basil, and mushrooms. Cover and cook on low 5 to 6 hours or until the venison is tender. After removing the venison, stir the heavy cream into the cooking juices and adjust seasoning with salt and pepper. Serve over hot rice or buttered noodles.

Serves 6.

Henry says: "Bursting with earthy flavors, and so tender it can be cut with a fork."

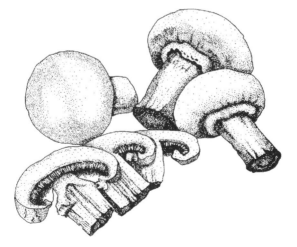

Venison Neck Roast

1 boneless venison neck roast, trimmed of all fat, rolled and tied
6 strips bacon
4 medium onions, chopped
4 stalks celery, sliced
2 15-oz. cans Italian-style tomatoes mixed with ½ cup honey
1 cup apple juice or sweet white wine
½ tsp. black pepper
1 tsp. seasoned salt
1 tsp. dried basil
2 tsp. granulated garlic
4 medium carrots, peeled and cut into ¾-inch pieces
6 medium potatoes, peeled and cut into quarters

Place the venison in a large roasting pan. Add tomatoes, onion, celery, wine, salt, pepper, basil, and garlic. Place the sliced bacon over the top of the venison roast. Cover and bake in a 375° oven for 4 to 5 hours, basting occasionally with the pan juices. Add potatoes and carrots during the last hour of roasting.

Serves 6 to 8.

Henry says: "Best if the venison is trimmed of all fat to avoid that overly-wild taste. If additional moisture is desired, add strips of bacon inside the roast before tying".

Leg of Venison Roast

4 lb. leg of venison, trimmed of most fat
4 cloves garlic, sliced
1 tsp. oregano
1 tsp. thyme
½ tsp. ground rosemary
½ tsp. salt
¼ tsp. white pepper
½ cup olive oil

In a medium-size bowl, mix together oregano, thyme, rosemary, salt, pepper, and olive oil. Let stand for at least 1 hour before using to allow flavors to develop.

Cut small slits in the surface of the roast and insert a slice of garlic in each cut. Place roast on a rack in an open roasting pan and brush with the oil/herb mixture. Bake in a preheated 375° oven for 1 hour; brush again with oil/herb mixture, reduce oven to 325° and continue roasting for 40 to 60 minutes or until internal temperature reaches 180°.

Serves 4 to 6.

Henry says: "Remove the shank from the roast and it will be sized to fit in most roasting pans."

Sautéed Venison Steak

3 lb. venison steak
1 Tbs. olive oil
1 medium onion, sliced
1 15-oz. can stewed tomatoes puréed
    with 1 Tbs. brown sugar
1 Tbs. red wine vinegar
1 Tbs. Worcestershire sauce
salt and pepper to taste

In a deep sauté pan, heat the oil and brown the steaks on both sides. Cover the steaks with onions, tomatoes, vinegar, and Worcestershire sauce. Cover and simmer over low heat for 20 minutes.

Serves 4 to 6.

Henry says: "Serve with mashed potatoes and buttered carrots. In a pinch, canned soup could be substituted for the tomatoes, but mix with 1 cup of water for proper moisture."

Poached Venison Chops

8 venison chops
1 cup flour seasoned with ½ tsp. salt and ¼ tsp. white pepper
2 Tbs. olive oil
1 cup white wine
3 fresh tomatoes, peeled, seeded and diced
1 medium onion, chopped
1 clove garlic, minced
1 tsp. brown sugar

Dust the chops with seasoned flour. In a heavy skillet, heat the oil and brown the chops on each side. Add the onions, tomatoes, wine, and garlic. Cover and simmer 15 minutes. Stir in the brown sugar and adjust seasoning with salt and pepper. Cover and simmer an additional 15 minutes.

Serves 4 to 6.

Henry says: "Serve with wild rice and fresh vegetables. If you like it spicy, add ¼ tsp. red pepper flakes. If you like a tomato cream sauce, stir in ½ cup heavy cream just before serving".

Venison Tenderloin with Wild Rice

1 lb. venison tenderloin, cut into ¼-inch-thick strips 1½ inches long
3 strips bacon cut into ½-inch pieces
1 Tbs. olive oil
¼ cup green onion, chopped
1 cup fresh mushrooms, sliced
2 cups cooked wild rice
½ cup white wine mixed with 2 Tbs. teriyaki sauce
1 medium-sized tomato, peeled, seeded and diced

In a medium sauté pan, heat the oil and brown the bacon. Reduce heat to medium and add the onion and venison; sauté until the venison is no longer pink. Stir in the mushrooms and wine; sauté another 5 minutes. Mix in the wild rice, cover and heat through. Toss in the chopped tomato just before serving.

Serves 2 to 4.

Henry says: "A perfect one-pan meal. For a variation, place the mixture in a buttered casserole, top with shredded cheese, and bake at 300° for 20 to 30 minutes."

Baked Venison Chop Barbecue

8 venison chops
1 cup of your favorite spicy barbecue sauce
6 Tbs. honey
¼ cup apple juice
1 tsp. tarragon
8 lemon slices

In a small saucepan, heat the barbecue sauce. Stir in the honey, apple juice, and tarragon, and simmer for 10 minutes.

Arrange the chops in a single layer in an oiled, shallow baking dish. Spoon sauce over each chop and top with lemon slices.

Bake, uncovered, in a 350° oven for about 1 hour or until the venison is tender.

Serves 4 to 6.

Henry says: "Using prepared sauce saves time and, frankly, if you find one you like, use it as a base for your own creations!"

Baked Breaded Venison Chops

8 venison chops, cut 1-inch thick
½ cup fresh parsley, minced fine
1 cup crushed wheat bran cereal
½ cup Dijon mustard
½ tsp. granulated garlic
¼ tsp. seasoned salt
dash of pepper to taste
½ an orange

 In a small bowl, mix together parsley, cereal, mustard, garlic, and pepper. Rub both sides of the chops with the orange. Press the parsley mixture firmly on both sides of the chops. Arrange chops in a single layer in an oiled baking dish. Bake in a preheated 400° oven for 8 to 10 minutes. Reduce heat to 350° and bake for 15 to 20 minutes or until golden brown.

Serves 6 to 8.

Henry says: "In our test kitchen, we found that the breading stays on the chops better if the chops are refrigerated for 1 hour after coating with the parsley mixture."

Chicken-Fried Venison Steak

2 lb. boneless venison steak, sliced ½-inch,
    flattened to ¼-inch thick
1 cup flour seasoned with ½ tsp. salt, ¼ tsp. white
    pepper and 2 tsp. paprika
3 Tbs. olive oil
2 medium onions, sliced
1 cup mushrooms, sliced
1 15-oz. can tomato purée, mixed with 1 tsp. sugar
1 cup heavy cream

Dredge the venison in the seasoned flour. In a heavy skillet, heat the oil and brown the venison on both sides; transfer the slices to a buttered, oven-proof casserole. Add the onions and mushrooms. Mix together the tomatoes and cream, season to taste with salt and pepper, and pour over the mushrooms and onions. Bake in a preheated 300° oven for approximately 2 hours.

Serves 6 to 8.

Henry says: "The cooking process can be completed on the stove top, but cover the skillet, use low heat, and check the liquid level often. Simmer until fork tender."

Hawaiian-Style Venison Chops

8 boneless venison chops
2 Tbs. sweet butter
1 medium green pepper, diced
3 green onions, sliced thin
½ cup pineapple juice or orange juice
¼ cup red wine vinegar
1 cup catsup
1 small can mandarin orange sections

In a heavy skillet, melt the butter and brown the venison on both sides; remove the chops from the pan. Add the green pepper and onions to the pan and stir-fry until brown. Stir in the juice, vinegar, and catsup; simmer for 3 to 4 minutes. Return the chops to the skillet, cover and simmer for 30 minutes or until fork tender. Serve over steamed rice.

Serves 4 to 6.

Henry says: "Very fruity-flavored sauce! For variety, add red pepper flakes for spark and a clove of mixed garlic for extra punch."

Venison Roast with Bacon and Onions

1 boneless venison leg
6 large onions, peeled and sliced
2 cloves garlic, minced
4 stalks celery, sliced
1½ lb. thick-sliced bacon, cut into 2-inch pieces
2 cups white wine
¼ lb. sweet butter
¼ cup teriyaki sauce
½ tsp. dried basil
½ tsp. salt
¼ tsp. white pepper

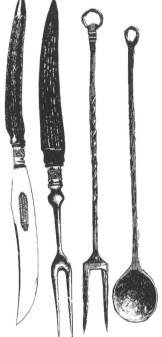

Place a sheet of heavy-duty foil in a roasting pan; foil should be large enough to cover and seal the venison, bacon, and onions. Place the venison in the roaster; season with salt, pepper, and basil. Add the onions, garlic, celery, and bacon. Pour in the chicken broth, teriyaki sauce, and wine; dot the top of the venison with dots of butter. Fold and seal the foil. Place roaster in a preheated 350° oven and bake for 3 hours or until meat is tender. Let roast stand for 15 minutes before slicing.

Serves 8.

Henry says: "Best if made a day ahead, sliced, refrigerated in the cooking juices, and re-heated. Before refrigeration, add 1 cup heavy cream to the pan juices and pour over the sliced venison. Re-heat in a covered baking dish at 300° for approximately 1 hour."

Roasted Rack of Venison

1 8-bone rack of venison

<u>Dry Rub Mix</u>
2 tsp. seasoned salt
1 tsp. paprika
½ tsp. white pepper
½ tsp. granulated garlic
¼ tsp. cayenne pepper

 Mix together the dry rub ingredients; store unused portions in a covered container.

Moisten the venison rack with a few drops of mild hot sauce (something similar to a hot wing sauce), dust with the dry rub mix, cover and marinate for 20 minutes.

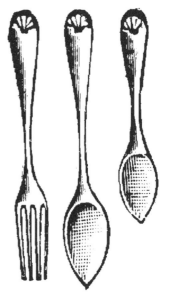

Heat your outdoor grill to medium-high. Cook the venison rack for 2 minutes on each side, turning each side a quarter turn each minute. Place the rack in a baking dish and roast in a 400° oven for 15 minutes for medium-rare ribs.

Let the rack sit for 10 to 12 minutes before carving; serve 2 ribs per portion.

Serves 4.

Henry says: "Simple and elegant, serve with fresh vegetables and steamed potatoes."

Grilled Venison Tenderloin

1 venison tenderloin cut into 8 equal portions
red wine
creamy Italian salad dressing

<u>Dry Rub Mix</u>
2 tsp. seasoned salt
1 tsp. paprika
½ tsp. white pepper
½ tsp. granulated garlic
¼ tsp. cayenne pepper

Mix together the dry rub ingredients; store unused portions in a covered container.

Moisten the tenderloin slices with a few drops of red wine and dust both sides with the dry rub mix. Using a spoon, spread the tenderloin pieces with Italian dressing, just enough to coat both sides. Cover and marinate 15 to 20 minutes.

Heat your outdoor grill to medium-high. Cook the tenderloin for 2 minutes on each side turning each side a quarter turn each minute. Tenderloin will be medium-rare.

Serve with grilled vegetables and mashed potatoes.

Serves 2.

Henry says: "This technique was created in our test kitchen. The Italian dressing provides both flavor and moisture for successful grilling."

Venison Sauerbraten with Gingersnap Gravy

4 lb. boneless venison roast
2 medium onions, sliced
8 peppercorns
4 whole cloves
2 bay leaves
1 cup red wine vinegar
1 cup water
½ cup cider vinegar
¼ cup olive oil
1 tsp. salt
2 cups boiling water
10 gingersnaps, crushed
½ cup sour cream
1 Tbs. flour

Place the venison in a deep ceramic or stainless steel bowl. In a separate bowl, combine the onions, peppercorns, cloves, bay leaf, vinegar, and water. Pour over venison, cover, and refrigerate for 3 to 4 days, turning the roast twice each day.

Remove the venison roast from the marinade; wipe off any excess moisture. Strain and reserve the marinade liquid, discarding the vegetables and spices.

In a large, heavy Dutch oven, heat 2 Tbs. olive oil and brown the roast on all sides. Sprinkle with salt and pour boiling water over the venison. Add in the gingersnaps and simmer, covered, for 1½ hours. Add 2 cups of the reserved marinade, cover and simmer 1 to 2 hours or until fork tender.

Remove the venison from the cooking liquid and keep warm. Strain the cooking liquid into a 2-quart saucepan. In a small bowl, mix together the sour cream and flour and stir into the cooking liquid. Heat the sauce over low heat, stirring constantly until sauce is thick and smooth.

Slice venison ½-inch thick, arrange on a serving platter and top with sauce.

Serves 6 to 8.

Henry says: "Marinated venison roast is a Black Forest tradition. Serve with boiled potatoes and carrots, and perhaps a frothy stein of beer."

Ground Venison

Venison Meatballs with Rice

2 lb. ground venison
½ cup cooked rice
1 egg, beaten
1 medium onion, finely minced
1 can cream of mushroom soup
1 chicken bouillon cube dissolved in 1 cup water
salt and pepper to taste

 Combine the venison, rice, egg, and onion. Form into 1-inch balls and place in a buttered baking dish. Mix the soup with the bouillon, along with 1 additional cup of water and pour over the venison.

Bake in a preheated 375° oven for 45 to 60 minutes or until internal temperature reaches 180°. Serve over steamed brown rice.

Serves 4 to 6.

Henry says: "A family favorite. Watch the kids eat them up."

Venison Meat Loaf

3 lb. ground venison
½ cup uncooked oatmeal
2 eggs, beaten
2 Tbs. dehydrated onion
1 chicken bouillon cube dissolved in 1 cup of water
1 cup catsup

In a large bowl, combine all ingredients. Transfer the mixture to a buttered 3-quart baking dish and form into a loaf shape. Cover with foil and bake in a preheated 375° oven for 1 to 2 hours, or until internal temperature reaches 180°.

Serves 4 to 6.

Henry says: "Comfort food that can be made ahead. Use leftovers for sandwiches, or make up a batch and freeze it for hunting camp."

Texican Venison Chili

2 lb. ground venison
4 Tbs. olive oil
2 tsp. salt
½ cup mild chili powder
½ cup brown sugar
4 Tbs. minced garlic
½ cup catsup
1 large red onion, diced
1 large white onion, diced
1 large can blended vegetable tomato juice
4 15-oz. cans stewed tomatoes
4 15-oz. cans Mexican-style chili beans
2 4-oz. cans mushroom stems and pieces
1 8-oz. can sliced black olives

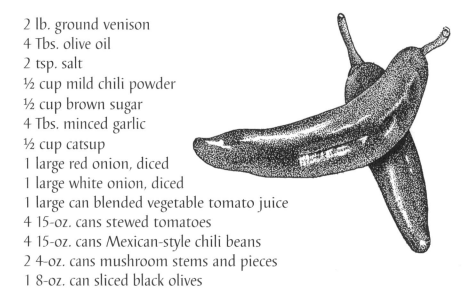

In a large stockpot, heat the oil and brown the venison and garlic. Add the brown sugar, chili powder, and tomato juice; simmer for 10 minutes stirring occasionally. Stir in the balance of the ingredients. Reduce the heat to low and simmer for 1 hour stirring frequently.

Cool the chili and refrigerate overnight.

Re-heat the next day and serve with crackers and beer.

Serves 6 to 8.

Henry says: "Always better the second day. If you like more heat, use a spicy chili powder and add chili peppers."

Venison Meatballs with Water Chestnuts

1½ lb. ground venison
3 - 4 Tbs. horseradish
½ cup bread crumbs
2 large eggs beaten with 1 cup water
12 water chestnuts, diced
salt and pepper to taste

Sauce
1 small jar orange marmalade
1 tsp. minced garlic
½ cup teriyaki sauce
¼ cup lemon juice

In a large mixing bowl, combine the venison, horseradish, bread-crumbs, eggs, and water chestnuts. Season to taste with salt and pepper and form into 1-inch balls. Place in a shallow baking pan and bake for 15 minutes in a preheated 350° oven.

To prepare the sauce: Using a 1-quart saucepan, melt the marmalade over low heat. Add garlic and stir in teriyaki sauce and lemon juice.

Serves 4 to 6.

Henry says: "The sweet tangy marmalade creates a wonderful surprise."

Venison and Mashed Potato Pie

2 lb. ground venison
2 Tbs. olive oil
1 large white onion, thinly sliced
1 cup mashed potatoes
¼ tsp. allspice
1 tsp. salt
¼ tsp. white pepper
prepared pastry for two crusts
1 egg, beaten

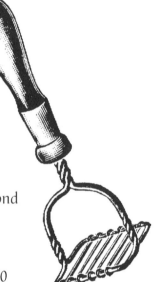

In a large skillet, heat 1 Tbs. olive oil and sauté the onions until tender; remove from heat and set aside. Heat the remaining olive oil and brown the venison. Remove from heat and stir in the mashed potatoes, onion, salt and pepper.

Line a pie pan with the bottom crust and fill with the venison mixture. Cover with the second crust, seal, and flute. Cut 3 vent slits in the crust and brush with egg wash.

Preheat the oven to 375° and bake for 30 to 40 minutes, until crust is golden brown.

Serves 4 to 6.

Henry says: "For a unique hors d'oeuvre, cool this pie to room temperature, slice into thin wedges, plate and serve with horseradish mixed with blue cheese."

Venison Lasagna

1 lb. coarse ground venison, cooked
1 lb. lasagna noodles, cooked al dente
1 lb. ricotta cheese mixed with 2 beaten eggs
1 lb. mozzarella cheese, shredded
3 - 4 cups puréed stewed tomatoes seasoned with 1 tsp. oregano
   and salt and pepper to taste
2 cups frozen sweet baby peas

 Oil a rectangular baking dish and spoon some of the ricotta mixture over the bottom. Begin with a layer of lasagna noodles, cover with ricotta cheese mix, ground venison, mozzarella, baby peas, and a thin layer of stewed tomatoes. Continue the layers, ending with lasagna noodles.

Cover the baking dish with foil oiled on the side facing the noodles and bake in a 350° oven for 1 hour.

Best to let this sit for 15 to 20 minutes before cutting. Serve with heated puréed stewed tomatoes.

Serves 6 to 8.

Henry says: "A great buffet dish. Add 1 lb. additional venison if you like a meaty casserole."

Texican Venison Lasagna

4 cups venison, cooked and shredded
2 3-oz. packages cream cheese, softened
1 medium white onion, peeled
   and chopped
8 green onions, sliced
2 cups Mexican cheese blend, divided
2 cloves garlic, minced
¾ tsp. ground cumin, divided
1 tsp. fresh cilantro, minced
¼ cup butter

¼ cup flour
2 cups chicken broth or bouillon
1 cup Monterey jack cheese,
   shredded
1 cup sour cream
1 4-oz. can green chilies, drained
¼ tsp. dried thyme
¼ tsp. salt
¼ tsp. pepper
12 6-inch tortillas, cut in half

Venison mixture: In a large mixing bowl, combine cream cheese, onions, 1½ cups Mexican cheese, garlic, ¼ tsp. cumin, and the cilantro. Mix in venison and set aside.

Cheese sauce: In a 2-quart saucepan, melt the butter, whisk in the flour until smooth, and gradually add the chicken broth, stirring constantly. Slowly bring to a boil; reduce heat; cook and stir for 2 minutes or until thickened; remove from heat. Stir in the Monterey jack cheese, sour cream, chilies, thyme, salt, pepper, and remaining cumin.

Spread ½ cup of the cheese sauce on the bottom of a buttered 13"x9"x2" baking dish. Top with 6 tortilla halves, ⅓ the venison mixture and ¼ of the cheese sauce. Repeat the tortilla, venison, and cheese sauce layers twice. Top with remaining tortillas, cheese sauce, and Mexican cheese. Cover and bake at 350° for 30 minutes. Uncover and bake 10 minutes longer or until heated through. Let stand 10 to 15 minutes before cutting.

Serves 8.

Henry says: "Serve as an entrée or as a football game hors d'oeuvre."

Venison Mediterranean

3 lb. ground venison
2 Tbs. butter
2 Tbs. olive oil
1 cup chopped onion
2 Tbs. minced garlic
4 cups peeled eggplant, cut into 1-inch cubes
2 large green peppers, cut into ½-inch strips
2 cups zucchini squash, cut into ¼-inch slices

2 cups sliced mushrooms
2 cups puréed stewed tomatoes
3 cups Swiss cheese, shredded
1 tsp. basil
½ tsp. salt
¼ tsp. white pepper
2 prebaked 9-inch pastry shells

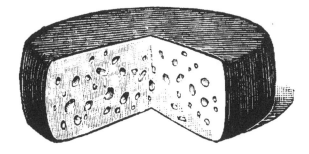 In a large, heavy sauté pan, brown the venison. Add the olive oil and butter, the onions and garlic, and sauté until onions are translucent. Add eggplant, green pepper, and zucchini, and simmer 5 minutes, stirring constantly. Reduce heat and stir in mushrooms and tomatoes, basil, salt and pepper.

Sprinkle ½ cup cheese on the bottom of each pastry shell. Fill each shell with one-half of the venison/vegetable mixture and top with the remaining cheese. Bake in a preheated 400° oven for 25 to 30 minutes or until crust is brown and the filling is hot and bubbly.

Serves 4 to 6.

Henry says: "Filled pastry shells may be frozen. If cooking from frozen, bake for 50 to 60 minutes."

Barbecued Venison Meat Loaf

3 lb. ground venison
15 saltine crackers, crushed
1 medium onion, finely chopped
1 large egg, beaten
½ cup of your favorite barbecue sauce
¼ tsp. celery seeds
1 tsp. dried parsley flakes
salt and pepper to taste

In a large bowl, mix all ingredients together. Press the venison mixture into a large, oiled loaf pan and bake in a preheated 400° oven for 40 to 60 minutes or until the internal temperature reaches 180°.

Serves 4 to 6.

Henry says: "Make a double batch and use the second loaf for sandwiches."

Venison Gravy and Biscuits

2 lb. ground venison
¼ lb. unsalted butter
½ tsp. granulated garlic
½ tsp. salt
¼ tsp. white pepper
¼ cup flour
2 cups heavy cream
1 can prepared biscuits, baked
   according to manufacture's instructions

 In a large sauté pan, melt the butter and brown the venison. Reduce the heat, add garlic, salt and pepper, and stir in the flour. Slowly add the cream, stirring constantly. If mixture is too thick, add a small amount of additional cream.

To serve, split a hot biscuit and spoon over a generous portion of gravy.

Serves 4 to 6.

Henry says: "Great for a stick-to-your-ribs breakfast with scrambled eggs, or a quick and easy dinner."

Venison Meat Loaf with Craisins

3 lb. ground venison
½ cup cracker crumbs
2 eggs, beaten
2 Tbs. dehydrated onion
1 cup craisins (dehydrated cranberries)
1 15-oz. can tomato sauce

In a large bowl, combine all ingredients. Transfer the mixture to a buttered, 3-quart baking dish and form into a loaf shape. Cover with foil and bake in a preheated 375° oven for 1 to 2 hours, or until internal temperature reaches 180°.

Serves 4 to 6.

Henry says: "Something special, festive and delicious."

Venison Meat Loaf with Peppers and Onions

3 lb. ground venison
½ cup bread crumbs
2 eggs, beaten
2 Tbs. dehydrated onion
2 cups sautéed onions and peppers
1 cup catsup

In a large bowl, combine all ingredients. Transfer the mixture to a buttered, 3-quart baking dish and form into a loaf shape. Cover with foil and bake in a preheated 375° oven for 1 to 2 hours, or until internal temperature reaches 180°.

Seves 4 to 6.

Henry says: "Serve with a hearty marinara sauce for a great Italian-style dinner."

Venison Meat Loaf with Andouille Sausage

3 lb. ground venison
½ cup uncooked oatmeal
2 eggs, beaten
2 Tbs. dehydrated onion
1 cup andouille sausage, casing removed and cut into fine dice
1 cup catsup

In a large bowl, combine all ingredients. Transfer the mixture to a buttered, 3-quart baking dish and form into a loaf shape. Cover with foil and bake in a preheated 375° oven for 1 to 2 hours, or until internal temperature reaches 180°.

Serves 4 to 6.

Henry says: "Very spicy, very Cajun. Serve with sour cream (it will help cut the heat)."

Oriental-Style Venison

2 lb. venison, coarsely ground
¼ cup peanut oil
2 cups celery, sliced
1 cup mushrooms, sliced
2 large green peppers, cut into ½-inch strips
1 medium onion, cut in half and sliced 1 - 2 inches thick
2 Tbs. teriyaki sauce mixed with 2 Tbs. brown sugar
1 cup chicken bouillon
3 cups cooked rice

In a heavy sauté pan, heat the oil and brown the venison. Add the onion and celery, and sauté until onions are wilted. Stir in the mushrooms, green pepper, bouillon and teriyaki/sugar mix. Heat through; fold in rice and remove from heat.

Pack the venison mixture in an oiled, 3-quart casserole dish and bake for 40 to 60 minutes at 350°.

Serves 4 to 6.

Henry says: "Add water chestnuts, pea pods, and baby corn for additional flavor and texture; a bit of crushed red pepper or hot sauce will give this dish added spark."

New England-Style Venison Chili

2 lb. ground venison
2 Tbs. olive oil
4 6-oz. cans chopped clams
1 large onion, chopped
3 cloves garlic, chopped
2 15-oz. cans diced stewed tomatoes
1 large green pepper, chopped
1 cup sour cream
1 cup heavy cream
1 tsp. hot sauce
salt and pepper to taste

In a large sauté pan, heat the oil and brown the venison. Add the onion and green pepper and sauté until the onions are translucent. Stir in the clams, garlic, and tomatoes; bring to a slow boil. Reduce heat to low and slowly stir in the sour cream and heavy cream. Add the hot sauce and season with salt and pepper.

Serve over hot buttered noodles.

Serves 4 to 6.

Henry says: "Sound like a strange combination, but trust me, it's wonderful! "

Crockpot Venison Sloppy Joes

3 lb. coarse ground venison
2 Tbs. olive oil
2 cups onion, chopped
2 cloves garlic, minced
2 cups green pepper, chopped
1½ cups barbecue sauce
4 Tbs. brown sugar
4 Tbs. vinegar
4 Tbs. Dijon mustard
4 Tbs. Worcestershire sauce
1 tsp. chili powder

 In a heavy skillet, heat the oil and brown the venison. Add the onion and garlic, and sauté until the onion is just tender. Drain off any excess oil.

In a crockpot, mix together the balance of the ingredients and stir in the venison mixture. Cover and cook on low for 4 to 6 hours or on high for 2 to 3 hours. Serve on bakery fresh buns.

Serves 6 to 8.

Henry says: "Great for Sunday football, or serve over pasta for a robust lunch."

Venison Cabbage Rolls

2 lb. coarse ground venison
1 lb. ground pork shoulder
1 medium onion, chopped fine
¼ cup instant rice
1 large egg, beaten
½ tsp. salt
¼ tsp. nutmeg
12 large cabbage leaves
2 15-oz. cans condensed vegetable soup
3 cups chicken stock

 In a large bowl, combine the venison, pork, onion, rice, egg, and spices. Mix thoroughly and divide into 12 equal portions.

Blanch the cabbage leaves for 2 to 3 minutes in boiling water, then immerse in ice water to stop any further cooking. Remove the leaves and carefully wipe off any excess water.

To assemble, place a cabbage leaf outside-face down on a cutting board. Place a venison portion in the bottom center of the leaf. Fold over the sides and roll; fasten with a toothpick or two. Repeat the process with the remaining cabbage.

Arrange the cabbage rolls in a Dutch oven. Mix together the chicken stock and vegetable soup and pour over the venison rolls. (Liquid should cover the rolls; if it doesn't, add water.) Cover and bake in a preheated 300° oven for 1½ to 2 hours.

Serves 6 to 8.

Henry says: "Add cabbage wedges and quartered small red potatoes to the cooking pot. Substitute white wine for water if additional cooking liquid is required."

Hunters Camp Venison Pasta Sauce

1½ lb. ground venison
1 medium onion, chopped
2 Tbs. olive oil
1 can cream of mushroom soup
1 can cheddar cheese soup
1 cup sour cream
1 tsp. Italian seasoning

In a medium-sized stockpot, heat the oil and brown the venison. Add the onion and sauté until the onion is translucent. Stir in the soups, sour cream, and seasoning. Simmer for 10 to 15 minutes, stirring frequently. Serve over hot buttered noodles.

Serves 6.

Henry says: "Okay, it's not gourmet, but it is an example of creating a meal from what you have on hand."

Hunters Camp Venison Stew

1 lb. ground venison
2 large potatoes, peeled and sliced
1 onion, sliced
1 stalk celery, diced
1 16-oz. can pork and beans
1 can condensed tomato soup
½ tsp. salt
¼ tsp. pepper

 Oil an oven-proof casserole. Layer potatoes, onion, and celery on the bottom of pan. Place a layer of pork and beans over the vegetables, followed by a layer of venison. In a medium-sized bowl, mix together the soup with ½ can of water and salt and pepper; pour over the casserole. Cover and bake in a preheated 350° oven for 1½ to 2 hours or until the vegetables are fully cooked.

Serves 4 to 6.

Henry says: "Another example of how to prepare a meal with what is readily at hand."

Venison Mostaccioli

2 lb. ground venison
¼ cup olive oil
2 cups onion, chopped
2 cloves garlic, chopped
2 15-oz. cans stewed tomatoes,
   chopped
1 cup green pepper, chopped
2 cups mushrooms, sliced

2 cups shredded cheddar cheese
1 cup red wine
1 lb. mostaccioli noodles,
   cooked and drained
½ tsp. salt
¼ tsp. pepper
1 tsp. oregano

In a large sauté pan, heat the oil and brown the venison. Add the onions and garlic and sauté until the onion is translucent. Add the tomatoes, green pepper, and mushrooms; stir and bring slowly to a boil. Reduce heat to low, add wine, stir and cover. Simmer for 30 to 45 minutes and remove from heat.

Butter a 3-quart baking dish and build a layered casserole beginning with a layer of sauce, then noodles, then cheese. Continue the layers ending with the cheese.

Bake in a preheated 300° oven for 45 to 50 minutes or until cheese is brown and the casserole is heated through.

Serves 6 to 8.

Henry says: "Hot and hearty; let stand 20 minutes before serving."

Venison Meat Loaf with Cheese

3 lb. ground venison
½ cup bread crumbs
1 large carrot, peeled and grated
2 eggs, beaten
1 medium onion, chopped
2 cups shredded white cheddar cheese
1 8-oz. can tomato sauce

 In a large bowl, combine all ingredients. Transfer the mixture to a buttered, 3-quart baking dish and form into a loaf shape. Cover with foil and bake in a preheated 375° oven for 1 to 2 hours, or until internal temperature reaches 180°.

Serves 4 to 6.

Henry says: "Comfort food that can be made ahead; any type of cheese will work, or perhaps try a combination."

Spicy Venison Meatballs

1 lb. ground venison
½ lb. ground pork
½ cup seasoned bread crumbs
2 eggs, beaten
1 medium onion, finely minced
1 clove garlic, minced
1 cup shredded pepper jack-type cheese
½ cup water
¼ tsp. cayenne pepper
salt and pepper to taste

Combine the venison, bread crumbs, eggs, garlic, onion, and cayenne pepper. Let sit for 10 minutes, and then mix in water and cheese. Form into 1-inch balls and place in a buttered baking dish.

Bake in a preheated 375° oven for 45 to 60 minutes, or until internal temperature reaches 180°.

Makes 40 to 48 meatballs.

Henry says: "Meatballs can be made ahead, cooked and frozen for future use. Freeze meatballs in a single layer on a tray; they store best if vacuum packaged."

Venison Salisbury Steak

2 lb. ground venison
¼ cup onion, minced
¼ cup green pepper, finely chopped
1 clove garlic, minced
2 Tbs. fresh parsley, minced
1 tsp. salt
¼ tsp. white pepper
¼ tsp. paprika
½ cup flour
¼ cup olive oil
¼ lb. sweet butter
1 tsp. Worcestershire sauce
½ tsp. dry mustard
1 15-oz. can stewed tomatoes, puréed
3 Tbs. Marsala wine

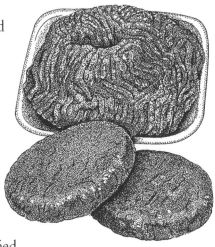

In a large bowl, mix together the venison, onion, green pepper, garlic, parsley, salt, pepper, and paprika. Form the mixture into 6 to 8 oval-shaped patties about 1-inch thick. Coat the patties lightly with flour, brush with oil, and either broil or pan fry to your degree of rareness.

In a 2-quart saucepan, mix together the stewed tomatoes, Worcestershire sauce, and mustard; add the butter cut in small pieces, and heat while stirring until butter melts. Before serving, stir in the Marsala wine. Arrange the venison patties on a heated serving platter and spoon over the sauce.

Serves 6 to 8.

Henry says: "A more formal way to prepare and present ground venison. For moister patties, add an egg to the raw meat mixture."

Venison Meatballs with Sweet and Sour Sauce

2 lb. ground venison
1 cup seasoned bread crumbs
1 envelope onion soup mix
2 eggs, beaten

 Combine all ingredients in a large mixing bowl. Form mixture into balls the size of a quarter. Place the meatballs on an oiled baking pan and bake in a preheated 350° oven for 1½ hours.

Sauce
1 cup brown sugar
1 cup fresh sauerkraut
1 jar chili sauce
1 cup water
1 15-oz. can whole cranberry sauce

In a large Dutch oven, combine all ingredients and heat, while stirring, to almost boiling. Add the meatballs, cover and remove from heat. Transfer to a heated serving dish or chafing dish.

Henry says: "Different and wonderful! The sauerkraut adds a special crunch to this appetizer."

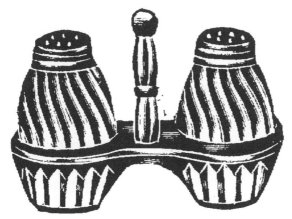

Venison Dumplings
with Bacon and Onion Cream Sauce

1 lb. ground venison
1 egg, beaten
1 Tbs. onion, minced

½ tsp. salt
¼ tsp. white pepper

 Combine all ingredients in a large mixing bowl. Form mixture into balls half the size of a quarter. Place the meatballs on a tray or pan and refrigerate 1 hour.

Dumpling Dough
3 eggs, beaten
2 - 3 Tbs. water
1 tsp. salt
2 cups flour

In a large bowl, mix together the eggs, flour, salt and water to make a smooth, workable dough. Divide the dough into 4 parts for easier handling and keep covered with a damp cloth.

To assemble the dumplings, dust a flat work surface or pastry board with flour and roll the dough to ⅛-inch thickness and shaped in a rectangle, sized at least 6 x 14 inches. Place venison meatballs on the bottom ⅓ of the dough sheet with about a 1-inch space between them. With a pastry brush, lightly moisten the dough immediately around the meat. Fold the top of the dough over the meat and, using the side of your hand, press/seal the dough between the meatballs. Using a cup or glass, cut the dumplings with each containing 1 meatball. Seal edges by pressing between your fingers or with a fork.

Drop dumplings into a large kettle with 3 - 4 quarts boiling water. Boil uncovered for 30 to 45 minutes or until the dumplings float. Remove with slotted spoon, place in a deep casserole dish, cover and keep warm.

Sauce
½ lb. bacon cut into ¼-inch pieces
⅓ cup onion, minced
3 Tbs. sweet butter
2 cups heavy cream

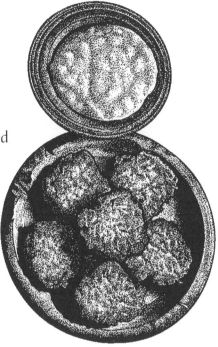

In a large skillet, fry the bacon until crisp; remove with a slotted spoon and drain on paper towel. Add the butter to the bacon drippings and quickly sauté the onion until golden brown. Reduce the heat, add back the crisp bacon, and stir in the cream. Heat but do not boil. Pour sauce over dumplings and bake for 20 minutes in a preheated 350° oven.

Henry says: "This recipe is Lithuanian in origin. It's a bit time consuming, but delicious and satisfying."

Miscellaneous
Venison Recipes

Venison Mincemeat

1 lb. course ground venison
1 cup currants
1 cup golden raisins
zest of 1 orange
zest and juice of 1 lemon
2 cups finely-diced, peeled apples
¼ cup white sugar
¼ cup brown sugar
½ tsp. salt
½ tsp. cinnamon
¼ tsp. cloves
¼ tsp. allspice
2 cups apple cider
½ cup candied citron, finely chopped
1 cup brandy

In a large, heavy stockpot, combine venison, apples and cider; bring to a boil, reduce heat, and simmer for 15 minutes. Add all remaining ingredients, except brandy, and simmer over low heat for 1 hour. Stir often to prevent scorching. If mixture becomes too dry, add additional apple cider. When cooking is complete, remove pot from heat and stir in brandy. Store in covered container in refrigerator for 3 to 4 days, or the mincemeat can be frozen.

Yields filling for two 9-inch pies.

Henry says: "Just like grandmother made, only substituting venison for beef, a much healthier alternative."

Venison Hot Sausage

8 lb. course ground venison
2 lb. course ground pork shoulder
1 Tbs. black pepper
1 tsp. white pepper
2 Tbs. fennel seed
5 tsp. crushed red pepper or red pepper flakes
1 Tbs. rubbed sage
2 tsp. onion salt
6 Tbs. paprika

In a stainless steel bowl, mix together all ingredients. Shape into patties or stuff into 6-inch casings. If using patties, bake in a 250° oven until just done (meat juices run clear); cool under refrigeration. The patties can be frozen on wax paper, and then packaged for storage. To serve, place frozen patties in a lightly-oiled skillet and heat thoroughly over a medium flame.

If you are using casings, freeze the sausage and wrap for storage. To prepare cased sausage, place frozen links in a skillet with water, cover, and heat until just cooked. Pour off any remaining water, add 1 Tbs. oil and brown.

Henry says: "Plenty of work, but the results are well worth the time and effort."

Venison Salami

5 lb. course ground venison
2 lb. course ground pork shoulder
1½ Tbs. course ground pepper
2½ tsp. garlic powder or granulated garlic
1½ tsp. barbecue seasoning
5 tsp. Morton's Tender Quick Salt
1½ tsp. hickory smoked salt
1½ tsp. onion flakes

In a large, stainless steel bowl, mix all ingredients well, cover, and refrigerate for 24 hours. Repeat the mixing and refrigeration process each day for 3 days.

Shape the venison mixture into 3 rolls. Place on an oiled rack in a shallow pan, and bake at 150° for 6 to 7 hours. Remove excess cooking juices as necessary. Cool the salami, wrap in plastic, and store under refrigeration. This salami can be frozen, and is best if vacuum packaged.

Henry says: "A great item for a Christmas or house gift. You can add additional flavor by smoking the salami for about 1 hour."

Venison Breakfast Sausage

1 lb. ground venison
1 tsp. oregano
¼ tsp. white pepper
¼ tsp. ground coriander
¼ tsp. dried mint leaves, crushed
¼ tsp. thyme
½ tsp. salt

 Mix all ingredients and divide into 4 patties. Over medium heat, fry until brown on both sides and juices run clear. Do not over cook or sausage will become very dry.

Serves 2 to 4.

Henry says: "For a variation, use the seasonings in this recipe for venison gravy and biscuits."

Italian-Style Venison Salami

12 lb. ground venison
3 cups water
4 Tbs. liquid smoke
4 Tbs. mustard seed
4 tsp. garlic powder
4 tsp. onion powder
3 tsp. dry mustard
3 Tbs. whole peppercorns
8 Tbs. Morton's Tender Quick Salt

In a large, stainless steel bowl, mix together the venison and 2 cups of water. Mix all remaining ingredients with the last cup of water and let stand for 30 minutes. Pour spice mixture over venison and mix thoroughly. Cover bowl with plastic wrap and refrigerate for 24 hours.

Shape venison mixture into 1 lb. rolls about 6- to 7-inches long; place on a rack and bake in a 350° oven for 40 to 45 minutes, or until the internal temperature reaches 160-165°.

This salami can also be processed in a water bowl-type smoker for 2½ to 3 hours, or until internal temperature reaches 160-165°.

The salami may be frozen after cooking or smoking, but is best if vacuum packaged.

Yields about 13 logs.

Henry says: "A lot of work but well worth the effort; it makes a great gift during the holidays."

Venison Sausage and Potatoes

2 lb. smoked venison sausage, sliced into ½-inch pieces
6 medium potatoes, peeled and sliced thin
2 small onions, peeled and sliced thin
2 cloves garlic, minced
2 Tbs. teriyaki sauce
1 cup dry white wine
3 Tbs. olive oil
½ tsp. parsley flakes
salt and pepper to taste

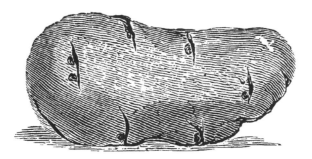 In a large Dutch oven, heat the oil and sauté the onions and garlic until the onions are translucent. Add the teriyaki sauce, wine, salt, pepper, and parsley; mix thoroughly. Add potatoes and sausage and stir gently. Cover and cook over medium heat, stirring occasionally, for 20 to 30 minutes or until the potatoes are tender.

Serves 6.

Henry says: "A quick and easy recipe for hunting camp, or for that home meal when you are pressed for time."

Venison Heart and Sausage Goulash

1 venison heart, veins removed, cut into ¾-inch cubes
1 medium onion, sliced
1 cup water
1 beef bouillon cube

1 lb. precooked sausage cut into ¾-inch slices
(smoked venison, bratwurst, your choice)
1 small onion, medium diced

1 lb. button mushrooms
1 can stewed tomatoes
2 fresh tomatoes, cut into eighths
1½ tsp. Italian seasoning
1 cup sour cream

 Simmer the first four ingredients for 5 to 6 hours on low in a slow cooker.

In a heavy skillet, heat 1 Tbs. olive oil and brown the sausage and remaining onion. Add the sausage, onion, and remaining ingredients, *except the sour cream*, to the slow cooker, and simmer for 1 hour.

Add the sour cream, stir and heat through. Serve over steamed rice or noodles.

Serves 4.

Henry says: "If you like a spicy goulash, try using a hot or spicy-type of sausage."

Venison Burritos

1 lb. ground venison
1 medium onion, diced
1 tsp. cumin
1 tsp. garlic salt
1 tsp. chili powder
1 8-oz. can tomato sauce

1 15-oz. can refried beans
12 oz. grated jack cheese
8 large flour tortillas
1 15-oz. can taco sauce
1 small can green chilies

In a heavy sauté pan, brown the venison with the onion until the onion is tender. Add the spices, stir in the tomato sauce, beans, and three-quarters of the grated cheese. Over low heat, continue cooking until the cheese has melted. Remove pan from heat.

Place a tortilla on a flat surface. Spoon about ½ cup of the venison mixture onto the tortilla, about two inches off center. Fold the bottom of the tortilla up to just cover the venison mixture, fold the ends toward the center and roll to make a sealed package. Repeat the process for the remaining tortillas.

Place the tortillas in a greased 9"x13" baking pan. Top with taco sauce, remaining cheese, and green chilies. Bake at 250° for 25 minutes or until heated through and cheese has melted.

Your choice of toppings can include sour cream, chopped tomatoes, lettuce, and black olives.

Serves 4 to 6.

Henry says: "A wonderful dish for that Sunday morning brunch, or to serve on an appetizer buffet."

Venison Sausage with Wild Rice

1 lb. venison sausage (If fresh, crumbled; if smoked, cut into ½-inch slices.)
3 cups cooked wild rice
1 medium onion, chopped
1 lb. button mushrooms
1 10-oz. can cream of celery soup
10 oz. heavy cream

In a heavy skillet, brown the venison sausage with the onion until the onion is tender. Add the mushrooms, cream of celery soup, and cream; stir over low flame until heated through.

Combine the meat mixture with the cooked wild rice. Place in a buttered casserole dish, cover, and bake for 35 to 40 minutes at 350°.

Serves 4.

Henry says: "I prefer using a combination of fresh and smoked sausage. The mixture adds texture and a wonderful smoky flavor to this dish."

Venison Bologna

15 lb. ground venison
3 - 5 lb. beef suet
½ lb. Morton's Tender Quick Salt
1½ Tbs. coarse ground black pepper
1½ Tbs. mustard seed
5 oz. minced garlic
1 Tbs. ground red pepper
1 Tbs. red pepper flakes
1 Tbs. poultry seasoning
1 bottle liquid smoke

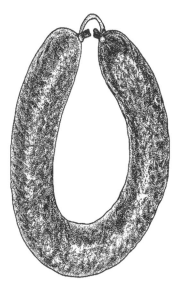

Grind and mix the venison and suet at least three times. Before grinding the last time, mix in all spices.

Stuff the meat mixture into casings and refrigerate overnight.

Cut the bologna into 8-inch sections and wrap in aluminum foil. Place in an electric roaster, on a rack, with water. Roast for 1½ to 2 hours, or until the internal temperature reaches 175°. Remove bologna from roaster and refrigerate overnight. Remove cooking foil, and re-wrap for freezing.

Henry says: "This recipe makes a lot of bologna; recipe can be downsized with very good success by dividing by four."

Fresh Venison Sausage

20 lb. ground venison
6 lb. ground pork shoulder
6 Tbs. salt
4 Tbs. sage
2 Tbs. ground black pepper
1 tsp. red pepper flakes
¼ cup water

In a large plastic or stainless bowl, mix together the ground venison and pork shoulder. In a small bowl, mix the salt and spices with the water, and distribute over the ground meat mixture. Mix thoroughly and grind one more time. Sausage can be formed into patties or put in casings. Best used fresh; does not freeze well.

Henry says: "Division of the ingredients by 4 will produce a more manageable amount of fresh venison sausage."

Philadelphia-Style Venison Steak Sandwich

1½ lb. venison loin, sliced across the gain ¼-inch thick
8 slices Swiss cheese
1 large green pepper, cut into ⅜-inch strips
1 large white onion, peeled, cut in half, and sliced ⅜-inch thick
¼ lb. unsalted butter
4 hoagie or hamburger buns

In a heavy skillet, melt the butter and sauté the peppers and onions until the onions are translucent. Remove from pan and keep warm.

Place the venison slices between sheets of wax paper and flatten the pieces to ⅛ inch. Heat the skillet to almost smoking. Add the pounded venison and fry quickly; salt and pepper to taste.

Split the buns in half, divide the venison, and place a portion on the bottom half of each bun. Place an equal portion of peppers and onions on top of the venison, followed by a slice of Swiss cheese. Cover with the top half of the bun and place under a broiler until cheese is melted.

Serves 4.

Henry says: "This is a habit-forming comfort food; spice it up with some hot peppers, salsa, or whatever trips your trigger."

Appetizers,
Side Dishes,
Sauces,
and Other Recipes

Cranberry Cream Cheese

1 8-oz. block cream cheese, softened
½ cup cranberry mustard

 Combine the cream cheese with the cranberry mustard, best if done with the aide of an electric mixer.

Place mixture in a serving bowl, refrigerate at least 1 hour before serving. Serve with your favorite crackers or flat bread.

Henry says: "This a favorite item in our restaurant, simple but elegant."

Marinated Shrimp

2 lb. 21-25 count cooked shrimp
2 medium red onions, thinly sliced
3 Tbs. capers
½ cup sugar
¼ cup Worcestershire sauce
½ Tbs. Tabasco Sauce
12 oz. cider vinegar
1 Tbs. salt
2 cups olive oil

In a glass or stainless steel pan, create multiple layers of shrimp, red onion, and capers.

In a large stainless steel bowl, whisk together sugar, Worcestershire, Tabasco, vinegar, and salt until the sugar and salt are dissolved, then slowly whisk in the olive oil.

Pour the mixture over the layered shrimp, cover with plastic wrap, and refrigerate for 24 hours.

To serve, drain the liquid from the shrimp, onions, and capers, and arrange the marinated shrimp on a serving platter.

Serves 10 to 12.

Henry says: "This is a 'trust me recipe' the combination of ingredients produces a wonderful product."

Spinach with Bacon and Onions

1 lb. spinach, washed and trimmed of coarse stems
2 Tbs. olive oil
3 Tbs. sweet butter
5 strips bacon, cooked and cut into ¼-inch pieces
1 medium onion, chopped

In a heavy skillet, melt the butter over medium heat, add the olive oil, garlic, and onions and sauté until the onions are golden. Add the bacon and spinach, cover and increase the heat to high. When steam escapes, reduce the heat to low and simmer until tender. Season to taste with salt, pepper, and lemon juice.

Serves 4.

Henry says: "The spinach cooks very quickly. Be sure and use fresh lemon juice to season this dish."

Thai Curried Peanut Sauce

2 cups peanut butter (your choice, smooth or chunky)
1 cup mayonnaise
1 Tbs. Thai red curry paste mixed with 1 Tbs. hot water

In a medium stainless steel bowl, whisk together the peanut butter, mayonnaise, and curry paste mix. Transfer mixture to a decorative bowl and serve with your choice of fresh vegetables (crudités).

Henry says: "This is a Thai peanut satay sauce that does not require cooking, and can be used straight out of the refrigerator without heating."

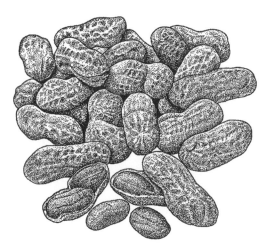

Bacon-Wrapped Dates

16 pitted dates
16 whole almonds
8 pieces thick-sliced bacon, folded and cut in half
16 round toothpicks
¼ cup teriyaki sauce

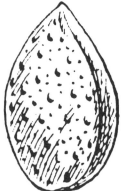 Stuff each date with a whole almond. Wrap each date with ½ slice of bacon and secure with a toothpick through the date.

Place dates on a nonstick cookie sheet and bake in a preheated 350° oven for 15 to 20 minutes or until the bacon is crisp. Remove the bacon-wrapped dates from the oven and baste with teriyaki sauce.

WARNING: Let the dates sit for at least 20 minutes to avoid burns!

Serves 4.

Henry says: "These are addictive. Make plenty, they taste like candy".

Crab Meat and Cream Cheese Canapé

1 8-oz. block cream cheese, softened
1 6-oz. container lump crab meat
1 cup picante sauce

Drain the crab meat and remove any remaining shell. In a stainless steel bowl, combine the cream cheese with the picante sauce, and then fold in the crab meat. Transfer the mixture to a serving bowl and refrigerate at least 2 hours before serving.

Serves 4.

Henry says: "Great hors d'oeuvre. Serve with crackers, cocktail bread, or your favorite vegetables."

Carrots with Pistachios

1 lb. carrots, peeled and sliced in ¼-inch coins
2 cups water
½ Tbs. sugar
¼ lb. butter
1/3 c Triple Sec liqueur
½ cup pistachios, shelled and skinned

In a large saucepan, combine the carrots, sugar, and water and bring to a boil over high heat. Reduce the heat to low, cover and simmer until the carrots are just tender, about 5 to 6 minutes. Drain the carrots and immediately add the butter. Return the saucepan to low heat and stir to melt the butter. Add the Triple Sec and pistachios and toss. Remove the pan from heat, cover, and let stand for 3 to 4 minutes before serving.

Serves 4.

Henry says: "The use of spirits with vegetables enhances their natural flavor and creates gourmet dishes from what would normally be very ordinary products."

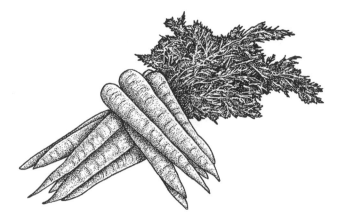

Acorn Squash with Cranberries

2 small acorn squash
¼ lb. melted butter
1 16-oz. can whole cranberry sauce
1 small onion, finely chopped
2 Tbs. brandy
pinch of red pepper flakes

 Preheat the oven to 400°. Wash and dry the squash, cut in half lengthwise, and scoop out the seeds and coarse membrane with a spoon. Paint the cut sides of the squash with the melted butter, and place cut side down in a shallow baking dish. Cover the dish with foil and bake for 35 to 40 minutes. Remove the foil from the dish and invert the squash.

In a medium-size bowl, mix together the cranberry sauce, onion, brandy and pepper flakes. Distribute the cranberry mixture equally between the squash halves. Return the squash to the oven and bake for 30 to 40 minutes or until the squash is tender. For added richness, add 1 Tbs. butter to each squash half before final baking.

Serves 4.

Henry says: "A wonderful side dish. To create a one-dish entreé, stuff the par-baked squash with a meat mixture, top with cranberry sauce, and increase the second bake time to 60 minutes."

Creamed Corn with Peppers and Onions

¼ lb. sweet butter
1 red and 1 green pepper, seeded and diced
4 cups uncooked fresh corn kernels or frozen whole kernel corn, thawed
1 large white onion, diced
⅓ cup heavy cream
pinch of nutmeg

Melt the butter in a 2-quart saucepan over medium heat. Add the peppers and onions and sauté until the onions are translucent. Add the corn, cover and cook over medium heat for 5 to 6 minutes, stirring occasionally. Add the nutmeg and cream, and stir until most of the cream has been absorbed. Season to taste with salt and white pepper.

Serves 4.

Henry says: "Comfort food, and a wonderful buffet dish."

Green Beans with Bacon and Onion

1 lb. green beans, trimmed and cut into 1½-inch lengths, blanched in
    boiling salted water 3 to 4 minutes and drained
6 slices thick-sliced bacon cut into ½-inch pieces
1 medium white onion, peeled and chopped
2 Tbs. olive oil
2 Tbs. orange juice

In a heavy skillet, heat the oil over medium heat; add the bacon and fry until semi crisp. Remove the bacon and drain on absorbent paper. Add the onion and sauté until brown. Add the green beans, bacon, and orange juice to the onion and toss to mix. Cover the pan, reduce the heat to low and simmer until the beans are hot.

Serves 4.

Henry says: "For an interesting twist, add 2 Tbs. Triple Sec – you will be amazed."

Kim Chee (Spicy Pickled Cabbage)

1 large head cabbage, cored, quartered, and cut into 1-inch pieces
2 large onions, peeled, cut in half and sliced ½-inch thick
2 large carrots, peeled and shredded
3 Tbs. minced garlic
1 Tbs. fresh grated ginger (optional)
2 Tbs. salt
2 cups rice wine vinegar
1 6-oz. jar kim chee base *
1 gallon container with a screw lid

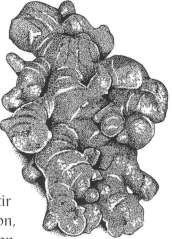

In a large, stainless steel bowl, mix together the vegetables, garlic, and salt. Cover the bowl and refrigerate for 12 to 24 hours. Drain the vegetables, return to the bowl, and stir in the kim chee base. With a slotted spoon, transfer the vegetable mixture to the gallon container and add the vinegar. Screw the lid onto the container and roll and shake it to mix. Store the kim chee in the refrigerator. The kim chee will be ready in 3 to 4 days and will only get better with age.

* If kim chee mix is not available, mix together 2 Tbs. garlic, 2 tsp. salt, 1½ Tbs. red chili flakes, 1 Tbs. sugar, 1 Tbs. grated fresh ginger, and 2 Tbs. red wine vinegar. Let stand for 1 hour, and then process in a blender or food processor until a smooth paste forms. If too thick, add a bit more vinegar.

Serves 4.

Henry says: "An acquired taste, but if you like hot and spicy, this is just the ticket."

Pan-Fried Sauerkraut with Bacon

1 pouch fresh sauerkraut, rinsed and drained
½ lb. thick-sliced bacon, cut into ½-inch pieces
4 Tbs. butter

In a heavy skillet, melt the butter, add the bacon and sauté over medium heat until the bacon is almost crisp. Reduce the heat to low and add the drained sauerkraut. (Be sure to squeeze out all moisture before adding the sauerkraut to the hot oil and bacon.) Cover and simmer for 10 to 15 minutes, stirring occasionally. When ready to serve, the sauerkraut should be a light nutty-brown in color.

Serves 4.

Henry says: "This is a family favorite. Add sliced apples for additional flavor and a little crunch."

Creamed Cabbage

1 large head cabbage cut in quarters, core removed, sliced into 1-inch pieces
3 quarts boiling water
1 quart heavy cream
1 package KNORR Hollandaise Mix
½ lb. butter
1 tsp. chopped garlic
½ tsp. nutmeg

 Blanch the cabbage in boiling water for 5 minutes; drain and place in a 2-quart buttered baking dish.

In a 2-quart saucepan, melt the butter and sauté the garlic until slightly brown. Reduce the heat to medium; add the nutmeg and KNORR Hollandaise Mix, then whisk in the heavy cream. Continue to heat, stirring constantly until thick.

Pour hollandaise over cabbage and bake in a 350° oven for 20 minutes or until hot and bubbly.

Serves 4.

Henry says: "You and your guests will be amazed at the incredible rich flavor of this dish."

Fresh Bean and Yogurt Salad

½ lb. fresh green beans and ½ lb. fresh yellow beans, trimmed and
   cut into 1½-inch lengths, blanched in boiling salted water for 2 to 3
   minutes and drained
4 Roma tomatoes, seeded and cut into ½-inch pieces
2 green onions, thinly sliced
1 cup plain yogurt
¼ tsp. yellow curry
1 Tbs. lemon juice
¼ tsp. salt
1 tsp. finely-minced lemon zest

In a stainless steel bowl, add the lemon juice and mix in the curry and salt until dissolved. Whisk in the yogurt; add the lemon zest and adjust seasoning with salt and white pepper to taste.

In a serving bowl, add the beans and combine with the tomatoes and green onions. Add the yogurt mixture and toss to coat evenly. Cover the bowl and chill at least 1 hour. Serve on shredded lettuce.

Serves 4.

Henry says: "A great salad for that summer picnic or barbeque."

Green Beans with Onions and Peppers

1 lb. green beans, trimmed and cut into 1½-inch lengths, blanched in
    boiling salted water 3 to 4 minutes and drained
1 medium green pepper, seeded and cut into ½-inch strips
1 medium red pepper, seeded and cut into ½-inch strips
¼ lb. butter
¼ tsp. oregano
pinch of white pepper
1 tsp. sugar
1 Tbs. teriyaki sauce

In a medium sauté pan, over medium heat, melt the butter; add
the peppers and onions and sauté until tender and slightly brown.
Add the oregano, pepper, sugar, and teriyaki sauce and stir to
combine. Add the green beans, toss to combine, cover, reduce the heat to
low and simmer until the beans are heated.

Serves 4.

Henry says: "Add chopped green onion for garnish and flavor."

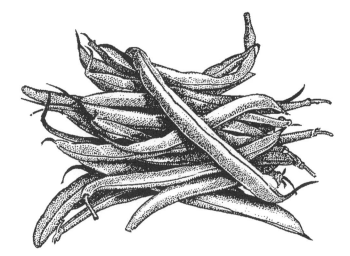

Lithuanian-Style Mashed Potatoes

4 cups diced red potatoes, cooked and bashed
1 large white onion, peeled, chopped, and
    sautéed in ¼ lb. butter until brown
8 strips bacon, cooked and chopped fine
½ cup shredded white cheddar cheese
⅓ cup heavy cream
¼ tsp. white pepper
2 tsp. salt

 In a large bowl, combine all ingredients and mix thoroughly. Place the potato mixture in a buttered oven-proof dish, cover with foil, and bake in a pre-heated 300° oven for 1 hour or until hot.

Serves 4.

Henry says: "A lighter version of a potato casserole called Kugula."

Mashed Sweet Potatoes with Apples

4 cups canned yams
1 cup apple sauce
¼ lb. melted butter
¼ tsp. pumpkin pie spice

In a food processor fitted with a steel blade, coarsely chop the yams. Add the applesauce, butter, and pumpkin pie spice and process until smooth.

Butter an oven-proof dish, add the yam mixture, cover with foil, and bake in a pre-heated 300° oven for 1 hour or until hot.

Serves 4.

Henry says: "I have tried this dish using fresh sweet potatoes, but the result is significantly better using a canned product."

Ratatouille

2 cloves garlic, finely minced
1½ cups eggplant, peeled and cut into a 1-inch dice
1 cup white onion, thinly sliced
2 cups green pepper, seeded and cut into ½-inch julienne strips
2 cups zucchini squash, cut into ½-inch slices
2 cups stewed tomatoes
1 tsp. fresh basil, minced fine
⅓ cup olive oil

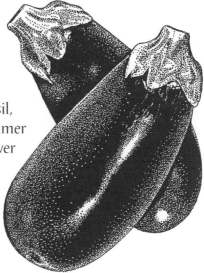 In a large sauté pan, heat the olive oil over medium heat; add the eggplant and garlic, and sauté until just tender. Add the green pepper, onion, zucchini, stewed tomatoes and basil, and stir gently to combine. Cover and simmer over low heat for 30 to 40 minutes. Uncover the sauté pan and continue cooking for 10 to 15 minutes to reduce the liquid. Adjust seasoning with salt and pepper.

Serves 4.

Henry says: "Serve hot with formal entrées, or serve cold or at room temperature for buffets or picnics."

Sweet and Sour Cabbage

1 large head red cabbage, cut into quarters, cored,
    and cut into ¼-inch strips
1 medium white onion, peeled, cut in half and cut into ¼-inch slices
3 Tbs. red wine vinegar
2 Tbs. water
2 Tbs. teriyaki sauce
1 Tbs. light brown sugar
¼ cup olive oil
½ tsp. salt

Heat the oil in a heavy sauté pan. Add the cabbage and onion, and over medium heat, sauté until tender, but still crisp.

In a medium-size bowl, combine the vinegar, water, teriyaki, brown sugar, and salt. Add this mixture to the sautéed cabbage and onion and, stirring constantly, bring to a quick boil. Reduce the heat to low, cover, and simmer until the cabbage is tender, about 5 to 10 minutes.

Serves 4.

Henry says: "For variation, add peeled and diced apples (Granny Smiths are the best)."

Zucchini and Yellow Squash
with Tomatoes and Onions

2 medium zucchini squash, sliced ¼-inch thick
2 medium yellow squash, sliced ¼-inch thick
1 large onion, peeled, cut in half, and sliced ¼-inch thick
¼ lb. butter
1 tsp. fresh basil, chopped fine
1 16-oz. can stewed tomatoes
1 clove garlic, chopped fine

In a deep sauté pan, melt the butter, add the onions and garlic and sauté over medium heat until the onions are golden brown. Layer the squash in the sauté pan, adding chopped basil between the layers. Add the stewed tomatoes, cover and simmer over low heat for 15 minutes or until the squash is tender.

Serves 4.

Henry says: "Try using purple basil; it has a pronounced peppery flavor."

Additional Recipes and Notes